For all those enamored by the Aveyron,

Recipes
from
the Aveyron

first édition

On filigrained art paper

The editor would like to particularly thank the painter Jean-Marc Valat for his beautiful watercolor, here used as the cover image.

From the same collection

Recipes from Provence, 2001

Philippe Galmiche editor
8 rue Rhin et Danube
12400 Saint-Affrique

ISBN : 978-2-912690-22-7

This book was printed on Vizille vergé art paper in the Aveyron by Grapho 12.

Recipes
from
the Aveyron

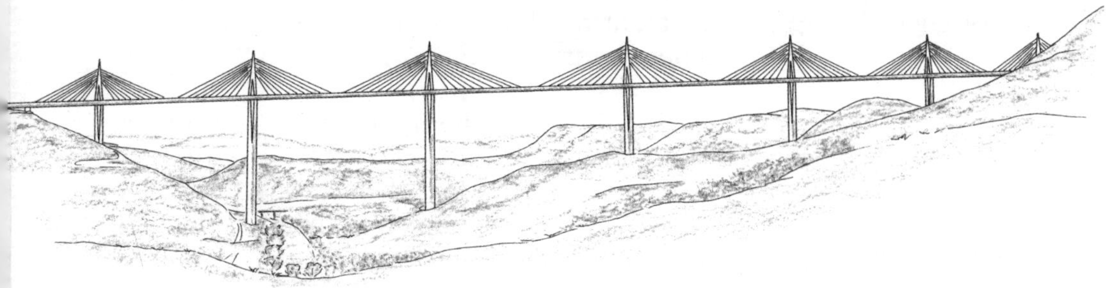

200 recipes compiled by

René Husson
and
Philippe Galmiche

Illustrations : Christiane Galmiche

Fleurines

Dear Reader,

Taste and inhale the cuisine of the Aveyron!

Eating is at the heart of the Aveyron. It is a sacred art and brings together a rich diversity of dishes and flavors, reflecting this region's diversity of landscapes. Perhaps you will find flavors from your childhood in the traditional pascades, the oreilletes, and the échaudés. Have you had the experience of turning the aligot during a family feast ? When it begins to ribbon the party «la festa» has begu! And have you tasted the pleasures of a breakfast of cheese soup after all-night reveling ? Or for the workers setting out for their day, a fumet des tripoux ?

The Rouergats didn't wait for the nutritionists' reports to add a bit of greenery to their farçous, to recognize the virtues of walnut oil in a dish, to enjoy the paradox of duck and goose fat, nor did they neglect the possibilities of beans, dried and fresh, wild and cultivated herbs, and delicious rye grains...

Share in the simple pleasures of a martrin and other salads, bajanac, tourril, and other soups, herb cake, stuffed cabbage, gratins, rosted duck, trout with verjus, fouace. Simmer with love a stuffed ase, an astet of Najac, a cabassol, a coufidou from Millau, a daube of pork trotters, a leg of lamb à la cuillère, white coco beans, confits, stuffed ham legs. Bring together in the best of ways, a hare and its sharp sauce, game birds' livers and juniper berries, veal and mushrooms, fresh cheese and potatoes, chestnuts and chocolate, strawberries and a fruity wine.

My dear reader, if you have never yet tasted a chicken with onions, nor rissoles, lean or rich, a spit turned cake, an estofinade, or a stuffed duck's neck ?
Then gather your tools and to work! A taula!

« The Rouergue
is one of those happy regions so blessed
by nature that it leads you to love
all life on this planet »

Curnonsky
Prince Elect of gastronomy

Before we cook

These first pages regroup useful information and techniques used in numerous recipes in one place. Check back to these pages as necessary.

Seasoning

Taste, check and perfect the seasoning of the final dish once the cooking is finished.

Bouquet garni

The most frequent components of a bouquet garni are a dried bay leaf, parsley stems, a branch of thyme or a celery branch. Don't forget to remove it before putting a sauce or soup into a blender or through a vegetable mill. Feel free to add seasonal and available alternatives such as leeks, a rosemary branch, chervil, tarragon...

Pre-heat the oven

Before putting your dish in the oven, preheat it for 10 minutes to the temperature indicated in the recipe. The following references will help you to find the right setting for your particular oven :

Low heat $< 120°$ C or $250°$ F
Medium heat 130 - 180° C (260 - 325° F)
High heat 190 - 240° C (350 - 450° F)
Very hot oven $> 250°$ C or $500°$ F

It is recommended that you try lower temperatures and a longer cooking time. A gentler cooking style better preserves the ingredients and their vitamins.

Cooking cabbage

If you would prefer to avoid the odor of cabbage in your home, add a tablespoon of vinegar to the cooking water.

Marinade

Use wine and vinegar resistant recipients. Avoid aluminum.

Preparing garlic

When preparing garlic « in its shirt » remove the green sprout at its center (this does not apply for new garlic). The sprout can lend a bitterness to the roasted garlic. For your vinaigrette, add the minced garlic ahead of time to the vinegar and let it cook a bit in the acid before adding the other ingredients (such as oil).

Preparing tomatoes

Tomato skins, be they cooked or raw, are undigestible. To remove them easily, lightly score the based with a knife and then plunge them into boiling water for a few seconds, followed by a cold water bath. The skin will slip right off.

When cooking tomatoes, you can remove the skin during or after the cooking time. This technique can save time and improve the flavor of the tomatoes.

Letting your cooked meat sit before serving

Meat cooked in the oven needs to rest, particularly red meats. This rule can also apply to oven-cooked white meats. Once the cooking time is finished, remove the meat from the oven, cover with aluminum foil, and let rest for 10 minutes.

Velouté

Putting a soup through a Chinese hat or a vegetable mill gives it a smooth and more pleasurable texture, as well as eliminating bits of vegetable skin, etc...

Ventrèche (Pork Belly)

The ventrèche is the pork chest meat, which corresponds to the lean bacon as it has alternating layers of meat and fat.

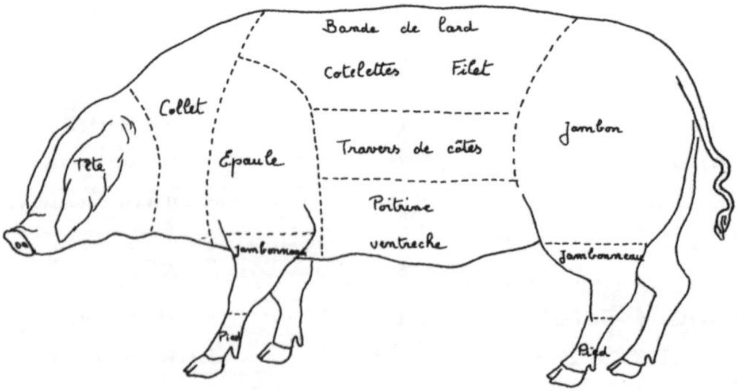

Making a brioche, bread or tart dough

When adding liquid to your dry ingredients, do it little by little as flours can have different absorptive powers, and you don't want your dough to become too sticky. But, do however, lean towards a more humid dough, than dry.

Pre-baking your pie shell

Be sure to press your pie dough firmly into the base of the pie pan. Using a fork, poke the base in multiple places to prevent bubbling during the pre-baking.

Kneading bread or brioche dough

Once the butter has been gently finger mixed into the dough, dump it onto a floured work surface and push the dough with the base of your hand, then fold the outer edge back over. Turn the dough and begin again. Continue till the dough is firm and smooth. Don't be afraid to do this for upwards of ten minutes. And enjoy the exercise!

Placing your pie dough in the pie pan

Once your dough has chilled sufficiently, cut out a circle of parchment paper the size of your pan, including the sides and the rim. Roll out your dough on this circle till it touches the edges. Slide both the paper and the dough into the pan, press in the bottom edges firmly.

Removing cakes and tarts from their pans

Wait 10 to 15 minutes before removal, then slide (or flip depending on the cake) onto a drying rack which will permit humidity to evaporate.

Whipping egg whites

Tip your bowl. Hold the whisk with the tips of your fingers to allow you to whisk with more force and movement. Whisk till the egg whites are firm and light.

Testing for doneness for jams and confitures

Use a cold plate. The jam is done when a drop on a plate doesn't run.

Filling your jam jars

Fill your jars to just below the lid. Put on the lid firmly and flip upside down. Once they are cooled, put them right side up.

Cardinal au marcillac

Per person

1 glass of red wine from Marcillac, nicely chilled
1 tablespoon of crème de cassis

Put the crème de cassis in the bottom of the wine glass, and pour the wine heartily over it.

The mansois grape is the primary grape in Marcillac. Cultivated on rougiers it makes the perfect wine for a cardinal with its lovely carmine color and red berry bouquet (raspberry, black currant). May the party begin!

Herb Cake

250g flour (2 cups)
4 eggs
40g flat leafed parsley (1.5 oz)
30g fresh celery stalk (1 oz)
1 pinch of thyme leaves
100g ham (4 oz)
100g smoked bacon (4 oz)
100g grated cheese (1 cup)
(gruyère is standard in France)
1 tablespoon baking powder
1/2 cup of dry white wine
1/2 cup of oil (olive, sunflower, grape seed...)
white pepper to taste

Chop the parsley leaves. Cube the celery coarsely.
In a mixing bowl, mix the flour with the baking powder, then add the eggs one by one, mixing as you go, followed by the wine and oil.
Whisk the mixture till smooth. Add the ham, the bacon, the parsley, the celery, the thyme, pepper and grated cheese.
Stir together and pour into a greased cake tin, (or non-stick).

Place in a medium hot oven (130-180C (260 – 325F)) and cook for approximately an hour. Check for doneness with a knife. Poke it into the center of the cake. If it comes out clean, your cake is done.

This colorful savory cake is best and easier to slice if prepared ahead of time. Cut in squares it is lovely with pre-dinner drinks. Or, as a first course, slice it thickly. This cake can also be frozen for another day.

Juniper Canapés

2 wild poultry livers (from pheasant, pigeon, guinea hen, woodcock)
a few slices of country bread
20 juniper berries
the roasting pan juices from the cooked game
80 g butter (1/3 cup)
salt and pepper

In a frying pan, fry the livers in a bit of oil for a couple minutes. Remove them from the pan, and in a small bowl, mash them with a fork with the softened butter. Crush or mill the juniper berries and add them. Salt and pepper, and add a bit of the pan juices. Spread on the bread slices. Grill in a very hot oven for a couple minutes.

Grandmother Marinette suggests : put the livers of your store bought free-range chicken and ducks in the freezer. They can be combined with your game bird livers to make more of this lovely appetizer.

Pig Rillettes (Fritons) for the year

2 kg (4.4 lbs) pork throat
5 hearts, 6 tongues
2 ears, and 6 kidneys
lard/bacon rinds
1 glass of Madeira
(1/2 cup - or as needed)
per kilo (2.2 lbs) of meat :
18-22 g (1-2 tablespoons) salt
and 1 g of pepper

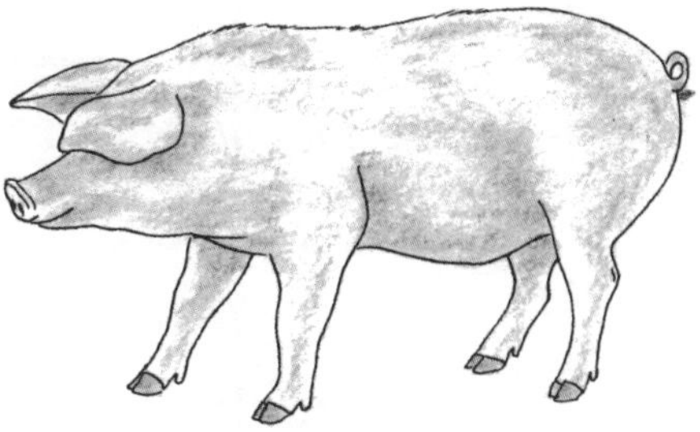

Cut the rinds, the meat and the pig offal in very small pieces. In a large recipient, mix everything together. Add the salt and pepper. Put into your sterilized jars, tapping them down well. Sterilize for three hours – If you don't have a machine for this, put the jars into a large casserole and cover with water. Bring to a boil. Let gently bubble for three hours. As the water evaporates, top it off to always keep the lids of your jars covered.

Excellent for salads, omelets, blinis.. or simply to eat out of the jar!
Preparing these «fritons» is an ancient tradition: they were made during the yearly slaughter of the pig. The bits of meat that stuck to the bones, and the offal cooked gently over a long period in their fat. Not too long ago, every Aveyron farmwife had her own secret recipe.

Fried Onions

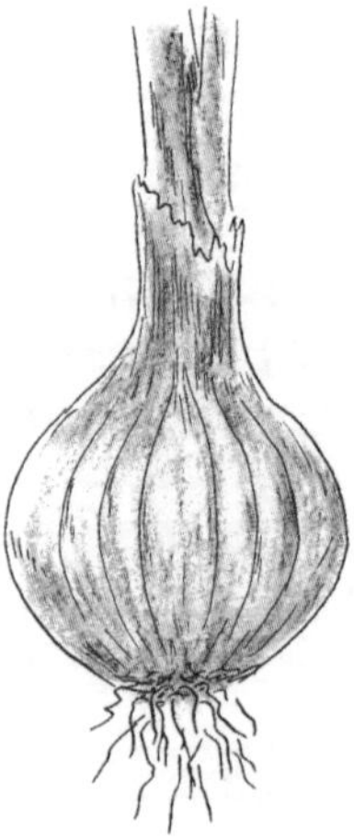

Large white onions
Milk
Flour
Frying oil
Salt

In a mixing bowl, mix together the flour and the salt. Slice the onions in rounds about 2mm (1 inch) thick. Separate the rounds. Dip them in the milk, and then in the flour mixture. Plunge the rings into very hot frying oil. Remove with a strainer when nicely colored.

Let them drip on paper towels before serving.

When served with pre-dinner drinks or to accompany meat dishes, there are never any leftovers!

Prunes with Roquefort

For 5 people

100g (4 oz) Roquefort (room temperature)
30 soft prunes (relatively large)
100g (2/3 cup) shelled and peeled hazelnuts
2 tablespoons crème fraîche (or cream)
1 tablespoon cognac
pepper

Crush (or put in a blender) your hazelnuts to make a coarse flour.
In a plate, crush the Roquefort with a fork, add the hazelnut flour, the cream, the cognac and the pepper.
Pit the prunes, and slice a small slit in each. Stuff them with the above mixture. Keep chilled till ready to serve.

Roquefort stuffed prunes and a cardinal for a pre-dinner drink. Isn't life lovely ? Prunes and Roquefort are often served at Christmas with walnuts, almond paste and chocolate from Bonneval.

Pickles in Vinegar

Small and firm pickling cucumbers
White wine vinegar, White pepper berries

Brush, wash and wipe dry your cucumbers. Put them in a pickling jar, add the pepper grains and cover with the vinegar.

Be patient for a month, and then enjoy these pickles!

Rosés des prés mushrooms in vinegar

Fresh picked rosés des prés
A sweet vinegar (honey or cider vinegar)
1 teaspoon pepper grains
salt

Rinse briefly under water, then blanch them for a couple minutes in salted boiling water.
Place them in a colander to drain, then gently tap them dry with a paper towel. Place them in a sterilized jar, add your pepper grains, cover with vinegar and close the jar.

Be patient for a month and then taste them. Add to salads, or put them on the table to accompany roast meats...

Roqueford filled Ham Rolls

For 40 rolls

4 slices of pork ham or shoulder
100 g (4 oz) Roquefort (room temperature)
1 teaspoon crème fraîche (or cream)
100 g (2/3 cup) vinegar pickles
pepper

In a plate, mash the Roquefort with a fork. Add the cream and pepper.

Wipe the pickles with a paper towel to remove excess vinegar. Spread the Roquefort in a thin layer on a ham slice. Arrange the pickles in a line down the middle of the slice. Roll up the ham with the pickles in the middle. Wrap tin foil around each roll, closing up the ends like a cigar, and place in the refrigerator for a few hours to chill.

Before serving, remove the tin foil and slice in 1 inch (2 cm) rolls. Place on a ham slice to serve.

These rolls are lovely to look at and to eat.

Semi-dried hard sausage in oil

500 g (1 ¼ pound) semi-dried sausage
12 ripe juniper berries
12 pepper grains
1 bay leaf
50 cl (2 cups) peanut or walnut oil

Cut the sausage in 5cm (2 inch) chunks. Put the sausage in a canning jar along with the juniper berries, the pepper, and bay leaf. Cover completely with oil.

Keep in a cool dark place for at least 10 days before tasting.

The sausage can keep for a few months this way. Saint-Affrique has a long tradition of pork products including sausages, hard and soft, fresh and dried. The charcutiers of Saint-Affrique date back to the 13th Century!

Poor Mans's sauce

50 cl (2 cups) vegetable broth
3 shallots - minced
1 bunch of parsley
1 drizzle of vinegar
salt and pepper

Over a low flame, pour in the vegetable broth into a saucepan. Add the minced shallots, the chopped parsley, salt and pepper. Drizzle a bit of vinegar over it all.

Bring to a boil and let simmer for 5 minutes.

This broth is the most common sauce for the common man, with its traditional drizzle of vinegar! In other times, this sauce gave flavor to the dishes on Fridays and Lent. Today, it is used to lighten rich dishes.

Roquefort sauce

100 g (4 oz) Roquefort
50 g (2 oz) butter
25 cl (1 cup) thick crème fraîche (or sour cream)
pepper

In a saucepan, melt the butter over a light flame. Add the Roquefort in small chunks. Let them melt while gently stirring. Add the cream slowly. Pepper and it's ready to serve.

Roqueford toasts

Roquefort, butter
Cumin, bread slices

Mix twice the weight of Roquefort to butter together, with a pinch of cumin. Spread the paste on the bread slices. You can put a layer of butter under the Roquefort/butter spread if so desired.

Divine toasts!

The Dolmen standing stones of Tiergues.
The Aveyron has the most Dolmen stones in France

Tomata

Ripe tomatoes
1 teaspoon of salt per 1 liter (1 quart) jar

Cut the tomatoes in half, press them and keep the fresh juice.

In a large pot over a high flame pour in a half glass of water and the tomato halves. You don't need much water as the tomatoes themselves will release their juices. When the pot comes to a boil, lower the flame and continue to cook covered for 5 minutes. Place the cooked tomatoes into a colander. Press hard to remove a maximum of juice.

Pass the tomatoes through a vegetable mill. Remove the water that floats to the surface and then put the puree into jars. Salt and cover.

Sterilize for 20-30 minutes begin sure to keep water over the cap of the jar.

The fresh tomato juice makes a lovely and healthful drink. Use the tomata for baking gratins, civets and stuffings (farçous).

Seasoned Tomata

Smooth out the tomata with some water, and should you so desire, some duck or goose fat. Add finely chopped garlic, parsley and thyme.

This makes an excellent tomato sauce.

Aillade

Garlic Soup

<u>For 4 people</u>

6 garlic cloves
1 bay leaf
4 slices of toasted bread
5g (1/2 cup) grated cheese
olive oil
salt and pepper

Bring a pot of salted water to a boil, add a pinch of pepper. Add the crushed and chopped garlic, the bay leaves, 2 tablespoons of olive oil and let boil for 10 minutes.
Pour through a sieve over the toasted bread in shallow bowls.
Drizzle a bit of olive oil over the top, and sprinkle cheese.

Served fresh and hot, this soup is the remedy for the mornings after feast nights. Garlic is said to help digestion.

Bajanac

Chestnut soup

<u>For 6 people</u>

1 kg (2.2 lbs) chestnuts
1 onion
1 liter (1 quart) skimmed milk
salt and pepper

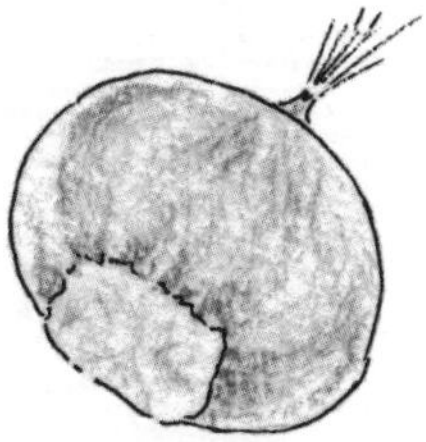

Score the chestnuts on their base and boil for 3 minutes. Remove both the outer and the inner shells. In a large pot heat the milk, the minced onions, the chestnuts, and salt and pepper to taste.

Cook for 40 minutes till well blended. Pass through a blender or use an immersion blender and serve.

If using dried chestnuts, soak them first in chilled water to soften.

Chabrot

aka Sabrot

Soup
Red wine

Pour a glass of red wine into your soup.

Any pretext is good for a chabrot. Traditionally it helps to finish off the last of the soup bowl. However others prefer to use the wine to cool the first bowl of soup.
Traditional Villefranchois residents play the game of «prisoner».
A cup of chabrot, a cup of soup, a cup of chabrot, and voila, our soup is prisoner to the chabrots, just like the prisoner held between two policemen!

Aveyron Stew (the simple version)

For 6 people

250g (9 oz) dried sausage - chopped
500g (1 ¼ lb) brussel sprouts
4 potatoes - cubed to - in/1cm in width
2 onions - minced
1 bouquet garni
2 tablespoons of tomata
or a tomato puree
oil
salt and pepper

In a large pot over a low flame, heat the oil and lightly brown the onions, then add the sausage. Add the tomata and the bouquet garni, moisten with the liter/quart of water. Add the potatoes. Bring to a boil and then add the Brussel Sprouts, salt and pepper.

Bring down the flame and cook covered gently for about 25 minutes.

You can replace the tomato puree with 2 chopped tomatoes and add them at the same time as the sausage.

Cabbage Soup

<u>For 6 people</u>

1 head of dark green curly-leafed cabbage
200g - 7oz of ventrèche/pork belly
6 potatoes - sliced in rounds
1 leek - the green cut in 1/2 in
or 1cm rounds, the white minced
1 onion - minced
goose fat or oil
salt and pepper

Remove the core of the cabbage, along with the larger outside leaves. Slice the cabbage in half rounds. Blanch in salted boiling water for 5 minutes. Drain the cabbage in a colander.
In a large pot brown the onion and leek with the goose fat (or oil). Add 2.5 litres (or quarts) water and bring to a boil. Add the ventrèche/pork belly, the potatoes, the cabbage, and the leek greens. Salt and pepper.

Cook covered over a low flame for about an hour.

You can add pig shank or pig knuckles for feast days. If you do so, extend the cooking time by at least 30 minutes.

Cheese Soup

For 8 people

800g (2 lbs) Laguiole
(cow's milk, from Rouergue)
cheese, preferably not too aged.
stale country bread
10-12 curly cabbage leaves
2 carrots - sliced in rounds
1 leek - sliced in rounds
(separate the whites from the greens)
1 tomato - peeled, seeded and quartered
1 onion - minced
a nugget of butter, salt and pepper

Remove the center bone from the cabbage leaves. Blanch the leaves in salted boiling water for 5 minutes and then drain in a colander.
In a large pot over a low flame, melt the butter and then brown the onion and leek whites.
Add 2 litres of cold water (2 quarts), the carrots, the tomato quarters, the leek greens, salt and pepper.
Bring to a boil and cook covered over a low flame for 40 minutes.
In a heavy casserole, place in successive layers, a layer of bread slices, a layer of the laguiole cheese in slices, the cabbage leaves, pepper, moisten with your vegetable stock and begin again. Continue till finished, ending with bread slices. Moisten well and sprinkle a last layer of the cheese.

Bake in a hot (190-240C (350 – 450F)) oven for 30 minutes. Serve hot, stirring the pot so that the cheese spreads throughout.

A traditional dish from the Aveyron for late evenings and parties. It is an authentic soup from another era, in which the spoon stands straight up! All the Aveyronnais partake of it. The more aged the cheese, the stronger the soup.

Squash/Pumpkin Soup with Chestnuts

For 6 people

800g (2 lbs) pumpkin/squash
500g (1 ½ lbs) chestnuts
1 onion - minced
1 leek - mince the whites, and slice the greens in rounds
1 half branch celery
1 bay leaf
oil
salt and pepper

Remove the outer shells of the chestnuts.
Bring a saucepan of water to a boil with the bay leaf. Boil the chestnuts for 5 minutes. Remove the fine inner shell from the chestnuts in batches, leaving the others in the hot water.
In a large pot over a low flame, stir the onion and leek whites in the oil till sweated (translucent). Pour in a liter and a half (1 ½ quarts) cold water. Add the chopped squash, the chestnuts, and the leek greens. Salt and pepper.

Cook covered for about 30 minutes. When the squash is tender put it through a food mill, or in the blender (but remove the bay leaf first).

This soup has the flavors and colors of the fall. You can use pre-peeled chestnuts which can be found in the freezer section at the grocery, or those preserved in jars.

Milk Soup

For 4 people

1 litre (1 quart) of milk
4 eggs
4 garlic cloves
(crushed or whole as you prefe
chives
1 bay leaf
4 slices of stale bread
salt and pepper

Pour the milk into a saucepan. Add the the garlic, the bay leaf, the salt and pepper. Bring to a boil and then, lowering the flame, let simmer gently for 10 minutes. Meantime, bring a saucepan of salted water to a boil, and hardboil the eggs in their shell for 8-9 minutes, then plunge them in cold water and peel. Mince and put aside.

In each shallow bowl place a slice of hard bread, and a portion of the minced hard-boiled egg.

Pour the soup through a sieve to remove the garlic and bay leaf.

Pour over the bread, and sprinkle chopped chives on top before serving.

Fava Bean Soup

For 6 people

700g (1 ¾ lbs) fresh fava beans
(or 300g - 3/4 lb shelled)
12 curly leaved cabbage leaves - chopped
5 potatoes - diced
1 onion - minced
1 leek - mince the white and
chop the greens - keep separate
1 branch of thyme
1 bay leaf
butter
salt and pepper

Put the fava beans into a saucepan of salted water. Bring to a boil and let cook gently for 30 seconds. Drain them and then pinch the outer skin off each with your forefinger and thumb.
In a large covered pot over a low flame, lightly brown the onion and leek whites in the butter. Cover with a liter and a 1/2 of boiling water. Add the potatoes, the cabbage leaves, the leek greens, the thyme and bay leaf. Cook covered for 20 minutes. Salt and pepper and add the fava beans.

Continue to cook for another 15 minutes.

This soup does not go through a vegetable mill, nor do you blend it smooth. Leaving the fava beans whole enriches the flavor and better fills your stomach.

Herb Soup

Sopa d'herbes

Templier chevalier au blanc manteau

For 4 people

1 litre (1 quart) fresh fish broth
250 g (2 cups) cooked peas
2 carrots - peeled and cut in chunks
3 turnips - peeled and cut in chunks
1 heart of lettuce - chopped and quartered
4 bread slices
1 teaspoon sugar
10 cl (2/5 cup) olive oil
salt, white pepper

herbs

1 branch of celery
1 branch of tarragon
1 branch of fennel
1 branch of marjolaine
2-3 branches of parsley

Chop the herbs finely.

In a large pot, place the carrots, peas, turnips and lettuce heart. Add in the herbs, salt and pepper, sugar and oil. Pour in 50 cl (2 cups) water. Cook over a very low flame for 1 ½ hours till the water has evaporated. Add the fish broth, let boil 15 minutes.

Check the seasoning and serve poured over the bread slices in shallow bowls.

A medieval soup with lovely flavors that bring back the days of the Knights Templar and Hospitaler.

Nettle Soup

<u>For 6 people</u>

1-2 handfuls of nettles
3 carrots - cut in rounds
3 potatoes - peeled
crème fraîche (or cream, or a dollop of sour cream)
salt and pepper

Wash the nettles and mince the leaves.
In a large covered pot pour in 1 ½ litres (1 ½ quarts) water. Add the potatoes whole, the carrots in rounds, the nettle leaves minced, salt and pepper. Bring to a boil and cook covered over a low flame for 1 hour. Mix and serve with a dollop of cream on top.

A fortifying soup much appreciated by the older residents of the villages for its numerous health benefits.
Pick the nettles before they flower-using scissors. Cup their tips at 30 cm (12 inches) to avoid the tougher lower sections. Wet nettles do not sting.

Green Soup

For 4 people

1 head of lettuce
12 spinach leaves
12 sorrel leaves
6 branches of chives
10 cl (1/2 cup) crème fraîche (cream)
1 nugget of butter
salt and pepper

Chop the lettuce, spinach and sorrel. Melt the butter in a saucepan and lightly wilt the chopped vegetables in it for 5-7 minutes. Pour in a litre (a quart) of water and bring to a boil. Cook covered for 20 minutes. Serve with the cream and chopped chives on top.

Tourril

Onion Soup

For 4 people

2 to 3 onions - chopped
4 stale bread slices
1 tablespoon goose fat
salt and pepper

In a large covered casserole, heat the goose fat and brown the onions. Pour in a litre (a quart) of water, salt and pepper and bring to a boil. Cook covered for 10 minutes. Serve very hot over bread slices in shallow bowls.

A soup quickly prepared and so good for you with all the virtues of the onion. In earlier times, it was accompanied with a fried egg baptized with the traditional drizzle of vinegar!

Jerusalem Artichoke Véloute

<u>For 4</u>

*700 g (1 ¾ lbs) violet Jerusalem
Artichokes - peeled and chopped*
*100 g (1 cup sliced) button mushrooms,
or girolles if available*
1 garlic clove - minced
1 liter (1 quart) chicken broth
oil
salt and pepper

In a large covered pot over a high flame warm the oil and brown the Jerusalem artichokes. Add the garlic and the mushrooms. Toss together over the flame for 5 minutes. Pour the chicken broth over it, salt lightly and pepper. Bring to a boil then lower the flame and continue to cook covered for 30 minutes.

Blend till smooth and serve with croutons.

A true walk in the Autumn woods! The artichoke flavor marries beautifully with the mushrooms, fresh or dried.

Martrin Salad

Potato and Chicory Salad

For 6 people

1 kilo (2.2 lbs) potatoes
3 good handfuls of chicory, dandelion greens or escarole
100 g (4 oz) bacon
1 large onion - minced
vinegar
oil
salt and pepper

Once cleaned, boil the potatoes in their skins in a large pot of salted water for 20 minutes. While still hot, peel and mash them coarsely with a fork.
Clean and shred your salad greens.
Mix together the onion, the potatoes and the salad greens, salt and pepper.

In a frying pan, brown the bacon cut in small pieces. Drizzle oil over the salad and top with the bacon. Serve warm.

The small village of Martrin, close to Coupiac, has given its name to this delicious country dish.

Cabbage and Apple Salad

For 6 people

1 half head of a green cabbage
3 green apples
1-2 slices of mountain ham (prosciutto can be used)
12 red grapes
For your basil dressing
1 handful fresh basil leaves
50 g (2 oz) fresh goat's cheese
4 garlic cloves
5 cl (1/4 cup) olive oil
salt and pepper

To prepare the dressing

Slice the cheese thinly. In a mortar and pestle, crush the garlic with the basil leaves. Add the cheese and crush till a smooth paste has formed. Extend the sauce with the olive oil using a whisk or fork akin to « building » a mayonnaise. Salt and pepper and chill.

Put your peeled and diced apples, the thinly sliced heart of your cabbage, the grapes, and minced ham into a large salad bowl. Chill.

When ready to serve, pour the sauce over it all, mix well and serve cold.

This medieval recipe from the Larzac is particularly refreshing and rich in minerals.

Gizzards and Walnut Salad

For 4 people

4 duck gizzards confit
1 head of lettuce
12 walnut halves
croutons
walnut oil
For the vinaigrette
1 tablespoon vinegar
2 tablespoons walnut oil
salt and pepper

Slice the gizzards. In a heated frying pan, pour in a tablespoon of walnut oil and toss the gizzards to warm them.

In a large salad bowl mix your green with the vinaigrette. Arrange the gizzard slices around the top, toss on the walnuts and croutons. Serve.

A delicious salad low in cholesterol that honors the many walnut groves in the Aveyron. These walnut groves used to produce large quantities of walnut oil. Happily, oil mills are cropping up again in Espéyrac close to Conques.

Dandelion greens salad with hard boil eggs

<u>For 4 people</u>

300g (3/4 lb) dandelion greens
4 eggs
100g (4oz) bacon - chopped
2 garlic cloves
croutons (small hard toasts or ideally from a baguette)
3 tablespoons vinegar
oil
salt and pepper

Hard-boil the eggs for 8-9 minutes in salted boiling water. Remove from the saucepan and plunge in cold water to cool. Put your washed greens in a large salad bowl. Rub the croutons with the raw garlic cloves.
In a frying pan, brown the bacon and top the salad greens with them. Deglaze the frying pan with the vinegar, salt and pepper.

Just before serving, pour the warmed vinegar over the salad, toss gently, and top with the sliced eggs, and croutons.

The bitterness of the dandelion greens is offset by the soft flavors of the eggs. In earlier times, dandelion greens were picked in the early spring to chase away the ills of winter.

Salade de "tenous ou grellous"

Baby cabbage salad

For 4 people

4 heads of baby cabbage
a few chopped parsley leaves
2 tablespoons of cider or wine vinegar
1 teaspoon mustard
4 tablespoons olive oil
salt and pepper

In a saucepan large enough to submerge the cabbage heads, bring salted water to a boil. Add the cabbage when it hits a boil, and lower the flame to simmer gently for 5-10 minutes. Drain.

In your salad bowl, put the vinegar and mustard and stir till you have a paste. Whisk in the oil, salt and pepper. Toss the cabbage greens with the sauce, and chopped parsley. Serve.

You can eat this salad warm or cold. In the Aveyron, baby cabbage (pre-flower) are called variously, tanes, grelons, grelhous. You can only find them in Aveyron kitchen gardens and occasional restaurants. They are lovely with bacon and/or hard boiled eggs.

Peasant Salad

For 4 people

1 curly leafed salad, or
dandelion greens, or Batavia
4 fresh eggs
100g (4 oz) bacon chopped
1 garlic clove, small toasts
1 onion - sliced
100g (1 cup) hard cheese – cut in sticks
walnut oil, butter
vinegar, salt and pepper
for the vinaigrette
1 teaspoon mustard
1 tablespoon vinegar
2 tablespoons walnut oil
salt and pepper

In a bowl prepare the vinaigrette: Put in the salt, pepper and mustard, and slowly drizzle in the oil whisking till it is the consistency of a mayonnaise. Add the vinegar to extend it.

Cook the eggs for 5 minutes in salted boiling water, then cool them in cold water and peel. Cut the cheese into sticks approximately the same size as the bacon. Rub the toasts with the garlic cloves.
In a small frying pan over a low flame warm the nugget of butter, and brown lightly the onions and the bacon.

Distribute the salad amongst four large plates or shallow bowls, then drizzle on the vinaigrette and sprinkle on the cheese. Slice off the top of your soft-boiled egg, cut into small bits to sprinkle on the salad and place the opened egg in the middle. Just before serving, deglaze the frying pan with a bit of vinegar, and pour the onions, bacon and vinegar over the egg. Garnish with the garlic toasts.

This salad is both beautiful to the eye and whets the appetite!

Bourriols

A thick and lacy pancake

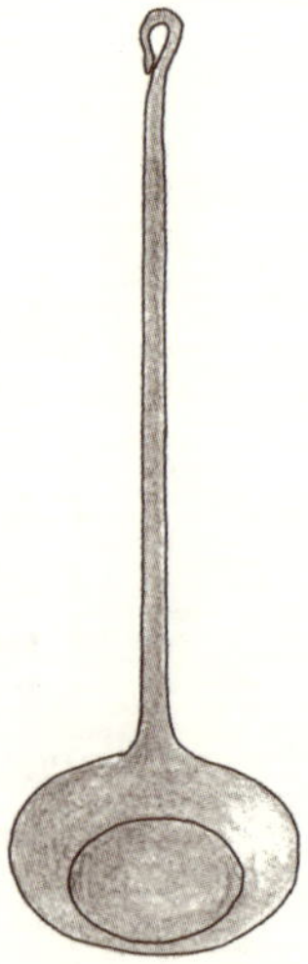

For 10 bourriols

250 g (2 cups) wheat flour
250 g (2 cups) buckwheat flour
1/2 l (1 pint) milk
15 g (1/2 oz) baker's yeast
oil

Warm a cup of the milk and stir in the yeast to test its activity. In a large mixing bowl blend the flours, the rest of the milk, and the now bubbling yeast. Extend the dough with a litre (a quart) of room temperature water. The batter should have the consistency of crèpe batter – i.e. very heavy cream. Let it rest under a dish-cloth for 4-8 hours depending on the temperature of your kitchen (longer in the winter, shorter in the summer).

Add another cup of warm water to extend the batter. Heat your large frying pan and pour in a tablespoon of frying oil. Quickly pass it under cold water, then place it back on the heat. Pour in a ladle of the batter and fry as you would a one-sided pancake.

The bourriols are typically cooked in a large frying pan, by preference an old one such as a « teule ». The rustic appearance of the frying pan and the cold water give the bourriol its characteristic laciness.

Farçou with Herbes

aka the " maigre " lean Farçou

<u>For 6</u>

1 kg (2.2 lbs) Swiss chard greens
or spinach, or dandelion greens
4 eggs
1 garlic clove - minced
1 onion - minced
1 parsley bunch - chopped
20 cl (4/5 cup) milk
100 g (3/4 cup) flour
oil
salt and pepper

Blanch the greens in salted boiling water for 3 minutes. Drain them and chop them finely.
In a large bowl, mix the greens with the parsley, garlic, onion, eggs, milk, salt and pepper.
Add the flour and stir till smooth. In an oiled frying pan over a high flame, pour in the batter, and cook for approximately 5 minutes. Flip carefully. Lower the flame and continue to cook covered for 10 minutes.
Check for doneness with a knife tip in the middle.

The farçou for Lent. It is now a dish appreciated for its healthy blend of eggs and greens..

Millas

250g (2 cups) sifted corn flour
1 l (1 quart) milk
1 tablespoon oil
salt

In a saucepan bring the milk to a boil with the oil and salt. Lower the flame and slowly add the corn flour, stir throughout. Continue stirring over the low flame for 20 minutes. The mixture will thicken and start to pull away from the sides of the pan. Spread it out in a serving dish.

If lumps form even though the flour has been sifted, whisk the batter to break them up. The millas is served hot or fresh from a frying pan, cut into small pieces. It is a delightful starch to accompany meats in sauce.

Sweet Millas

Use the same recipe as above, once chilled cut the millas into slices about a centimeter (1/2 inch) thick, toast them in the frying pan and serve hot sprinkled with sugar.

This is a nourishing and yummy dessert or snack for kids!

Pascade

200 g (1 ½ cups) flour
3 eggs
milk, water, oil and salt

Mix together the flour, salt and eggs. Add the milk little by little, then some water. Mix with a whisk to make a fluid batter with no lumps, about the thickness of crèpe batter or heavy cream. Let rest for one hour.

Heat a frying pan, add the oil and pour in the batter. Cook each side for approximately four minutes.

Pascade with Onions

200 g (1 ½ cups) flour
3 eggs
2 onions
milk, water, oil and salt

Mince the onions and lightly brown them in oil. Once they are golden, follow the above recipe adding the onions to the dough.

The Pascade is a Rouergate specialty that used to be prepared without milk, just water. It is for the lean times of Lent and Fridays and does not have any animal fat.

Picaucels

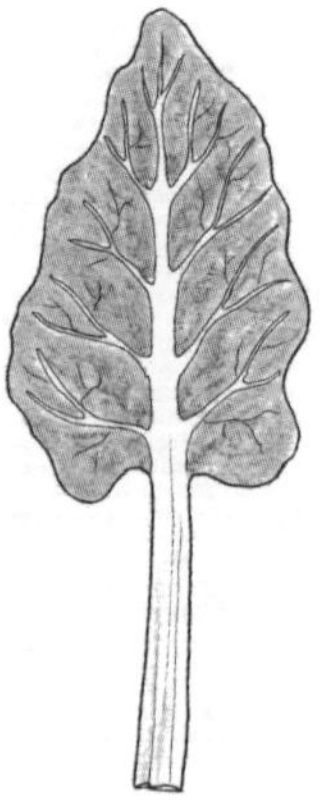

400 g (3 cups) flour
150 g (one cup) prunes
150 g (5 ½ oz) Swiss chard greens - chopped
4 eggs
40 cl (1 ¾ cups) milk
1 parsley bunch - chopped
1 tablespoon baking powder
red wine
salt

Blanch the swiss chard greens in salted boiling water for 3 minutes, then drain. Soak the prunes in the red wine.
In a large bowl, blend together the flour, the yeast, and the salt. Add the eggs one by one, then the milk.
Drain the prunes, then add them, along with the parsley and swiss chard greens. Pour the batter into a greased cake pan.

Bake for 40 minutes in a hot (190-240C (350 – 450F)) oven.

The picaucel is eaten as a savory dish, and you can enrich it with ham. It can also be eaten sweet by adding diced pears to the ingredients.

Green Pizza from Aubrac

For the pizza dough
400 g (3 cups) flour
240 ml (1 cup) water
4 tablespoons olive oil
1 packet of baker's yeast
1 teaspoon salt
for the topping
400 g (1 lb) Swiss chard greens
1 small cup of tomato sauce
150 g (1 ½ cups) fresh tome (hard) cheese from the Aubrac
50 g (1/2 cup) grated cheese (a gruyère is fine here)
olive oil and salt

In a mixing bowl, pour in the flour, the oil, the salt, the yeast, and then the warmed water. Mix together and knead the dough till it is smooth and elastic. Let rest.
Meantime, wilt the greens in a frying pan with the olive oil, salt them, and cook gently for 15 minutes. Remove from the pan and chop.
If you have a pizza stone, you can use it here. If not, one trick is to use parchment paper on your oven tray. Roll out the dough onto the paper. Spread the tomato sauce over the dough, salt, sprinkle on the greens, then the cheese.
Place in a hot (190-240C (350 – 450F)) oven for 15 minutes. Add the tome to the top after dicing it. Drizzle with a bit of oil and serve.

This pizza has the colors of the Aubrac, and is delicious ! Vegetable and cheese tarts, precursors to pizza, were already a staple in twelfth century Occitanie's communal ovens.

Eggplant with Cream

Aubergines with Cream

<u>For 6 people</u>

1 kg (2.2 lbs) not too fat eggplant (aubergines)
50 cl (2 cups) crème fraîche (heavy cream or sour cream by preference)
200 g (7 oz) smoked bacon chopped finely
3 garlic cloves
3 onions - sliced
1 bunch flat-leafed parsley
olive oil
salt and pepper

Slice the eggplant into one centimeter (half inch) slices lengthwise, layer with salt in a non-reactive dish and leave for at least 30 minutes.
Meantime, brown the onions and bacon in oil for 10 minutes, put aside. Mince the garlic and chop the parsley, put aside.
Rinse and dry the eggplant (in fresh water and between two dish towels respectively). Put more oil in the frying pan and lightly brown the eggplant slices.
Using a gratin dish, place a layer of the eggplant, then the onion and bacon mixture, then the parsley-garlic mixture. Salt and pepper. Place another layer of each. Salt and pepper.

Cover with the cream and put it into a medium heat (130-180C (260 – 325F)) oven for 20 minutes.

A tender and savory dish from the Eastern region of the Tarn.

Stuffed Cèpes

Boletus mushrooms

For 6 people

6 lovely cèpes
250g (1 ¼ cup) sausage meat
1 egg
2 garlic cloves - chopped
2 shallots - minced
1 parsley bunch - chopped
white wine
butter
salt and pepper

Clean the mushrooms and separate the caps from the stems. Slice a thin bit off the cap to allow for more stability when upside down. Dig out the inside of the cap (gently).
Finely chop the mushroom bits removed from the caps along with the stems. In a large bowl, mix together the shallots, garlic, chopped mushrooms, chopped parsley, raw egg and sausage meat. Salt and pepper.
Garnish each mushroom cap with a small ball of the stuffing.

Lay the caps on a buttered dish and bake in a medium hot (130-180C (260 – 325F)) oven for 50 minutes, basting with white wine every so often.

A gourmand's delight!

Stuffed Cabbage

Poule verte

For 6 people

1 lovely head of dark green curly leaf cabbage
500 g (1 ¼ lb) leftover meat or sausage meat
300 g (3/4 lb) Swiss chard greens
1 egg
2 garlic cloves - chopped finely
1 onion - minced
1 bunch of parsley - chopped
a bouquet garni
50 g (2 oz) old bread
milk
1 l (1 quart) vegetable broth
oil, salt and pepper

Remove the outer leaves from the cabbage and remove the center stem with the tip of a knife. Blanch the cabbage in a large pot of salted boiling water for 10 minutes. Drain.
Blanch the Swiss chard greens for three minutes. Drain.
Put the bread in a plate with the milk and let it sponge it up.
In a frying pan, brown the onion and garlic in oil, add the meat/ sausage and cook for 5-10 minutes, stirring to brown all sides.
Put the mixture into a mixing bowl, add the bread, the egg, the chard greens, the parsley, salt and pepper. Mix all together (use your hands or a wooden spoon).
Put a ball of the stuffing into the middle of the cabbage, and throughout between the leaves. Tie it all together with string.

In a large pot with a lid, over a low flame, place the bouquet garni and the vegetable broth. Bring to a simmer and delicately put the cabbage into the liquid. Let cook covered for 1 ½ hours over a very low flame.

Stuffed Cabbage "au pounti"

<u>For 6 people</u>

1 lovely head of dark green
  curly leaf cabbage
bacon strips
pounti (see page 147)

Remove the outer leaves of the cabbage, and the inside stem with the point of a knife.
Blanch the cabbage in a large saucepan with salted boiling water for 10 minutes. Drain
Garnish the heart of the cabbage with the pounti and put this throughout between the leaves as well. Wrap the bacon strips around the cabbage to keep the pounti from leaking out. Tie together.
Put the cabbage into a greased oven dish. Bake at medium heat (130-180C (260 – 325F)) for 1 ½ hours.

If you have leftovers of this dish, do as our grandmothers did, cut the stuffed cabbage in finger thick slices and fry on both sides. A true pleasure!

Swiss Chard stems

Côtes de blettes

For 4 people

600 g (1 ½ lbs) Swiss chard stems
4 tablespoons tomata (or tomato puree)
parsley
100 g (1 cup) pitted green olives
1 tablespoon olive oil
salt and pepper

Wash the Swiss chard and cut the stems into short lengths. Cook them in boiling water or steam them for 10 minutes (approx.) or till tender.
In a frying pan with high sides, heat the oil, and add the Swiss chard. Toss, then add the tomato paste. Sprinkle on the chopped parsley, along with the quartered. Salt and pepper.

Continue to cook covered over a low flame for 5 minutes.

Everything is good in Swiss chard! The greens bring a delicate touch to the family of «farçous» and the stems can be made into a gratin, a soup, or sautéed as here above.

Rice Stuffed Zucchini/courgettes

For 4 people

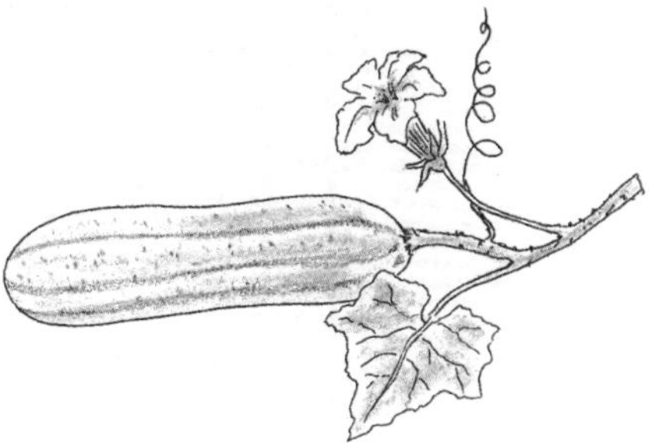

8 small zucchini/courgettes
50 g (1/2 cup) long grain rice
150 g (5 oz) smoked bacon
- chopped
1 egg
1 garlic clove - chopped
1 onion - minced
100 g (1 cup) grated cheese (such as gruyère)
olive oil
salt and pepper

Blanch the zucchini/courgettes in salted boiling water for 5 minutes, drain and cut in half lengthwise. With a small spoon, scoop out the center and put aside.
In a saucepan over a low flame, bring a 1/2 l (1 pt) salted water to a boil, pour in the rice and cook over a low flame for 15 minutes.
Drain the rice in a colander.
In a frying pan over a low flame, brown the onion, bacon, garlic and the zucchini/courgette centers (likewise chopped coarsely). Stir for 5-8 minutes, salt and pepper and mix in the rice.
In a bowl, mix together the egg and the grated cheese. Stuff the zucchini with the rice mixture, pour the egg and cheese mixture over the top and drizzle each with a bit of olive oil.
Bake in a hot oven (190-240C (350 – 450F)) for 20 minutes.

A recipe pleasing to both to the eyes and the palate. Select small zucchini/courgettes, as they are more tender and have fewer seeds.

Fava Beans with Bacon

1 kg (2.2 lbs) fresh fava beans (400 g, 1 lb if shelled)
100 g (4 oz) smoked bacon - chopped
1 garlic clove
1 onion - minced
1 bunch of parsley
50 g (3tbspns) butter
olive oil
salt and pepper

Put your shelled fava beans into lightly salted water. Bring to a boil and cook for 5 minutes. Remove the outside skin of each bean by pinching them between your thumb and index finger.
Make a « persillade » mixture by chopping together the parsley leaves and the garlic.
In a pot with a lid, over a low flame, brown the onion and bacon in olive oil. Add the fava beans, a 1/3 cup of water, salt and pepper. Mix all together and sprinkle on the persillade. Cover and cook very gently for 10 minutes till the beans are tender.
Serve with the butter stirred into the beans.

Enjoy this dish hot, warm or cold as a very nourishing salad.

New Fava beans with salt

If you are able to get your fava beans right off the plant, enjoy the very first ones freshly out of the shell. Each guest opens his own bean and dips it in the bowls of salt made available by the host.

This is a traditional regional pleasure for the months of May and June.

Potato Pancakes "au laguiole"

For 6 people

800 g (2 lbs) potatoes
(preferably the varieties BF15 or bintje)
6 eggs
150 g (1 ½ cups) laguiole cheese grated
2 onions - minced
1 bunch of parsley - chopped
2 tablespoons flour
oil
salt and pepper

In a frying pan over a low flame, lightly brown the onions in oil.
Peel and grate the potatoes.
In a mixing bowl, mix the potatoes, the grated cheese, the chopped parsley, the eggs one by one, the flour, the salt and pepper, and the onions.
Put more oil into the frying pan. Ladle in the potato pancake mixture, and spread it around to obtain a 2 cm (1 in) thick pancake the size of your pan. Cook covered for 12 minutes over a low to medium flame. Using a spatula, un-stick the pancake from the pan, and, with a lid or another plate, flip the pancake to cook the other side.
Cook covered for another 12 minutes. Serve.

The Roquefort sauce is excellent with this dish.

Broccoli Gratin

<u>For 5 people</u>

1 head of broccoli
500g (1 ¼ lb) left-over meat or ground cooked meat
2 eggs
1 garlic clove - chopped
1 onion - minced
1 small bunch of parsley - chopped
20cl (4/5 cup) tomato sauce or
seasoned tomata (see recipe)
80g (1 cup) stale bread
100g (1 cup) grated cheese
olive oil
salt and pepper

Soak the bread in a bit of milk.
In a frying pan, lightly brown the onion in oil, add in the meat and stir till lightly browned. Remove from heat.
Meantime, steam the broccoli for 8 minutes (or boil if you prefer).
In a mixing bowl, blend together the browned meat and onions, the bread (which you've squeezed out like a sponge and shredded), the chopped garlic and parsley, salt and pepper. Add the eggs one by one, mixing between.
In a gratin dish, oil the bottom, and put a layer of broccoli, then a layer of the stuffing, then a layer of broccoli, and cover with the tomato sauce.

Sprinkle the cheese on top, and bake in a hot oven (190-240C (350 – 450F)) for 20 minutes.

You can replace the day-old meat with fresh sausage meat. If you do so, double the baking time.

Cauliflower Gratin

For 4 people

1 cauliflower
2 scrapes on a grater of nutmeg
40g flour
bread crumbs
30g (2 tblspns plus a bit) butter
50cl (2 cups) milk
10cl (a short half cup) crème fraîche
(you can use cream or sour cream in its place)
100g (1 cup) grated cheese
salt and pepper

Cut the cauliflower into small flowerettes, removing the heavy center stem. Blanch in boiling salted water for 10 minutes. In a saucepan, melt the butter, add the flour and let thicken just a bit while stirring. Slowly pour in the milk, whisking all the while. Sprinkle in the nutmeg, salt and pepper. Continue cooking and turning till the sauce thickens.
Remove from the heat and add in the cream.
Using an oven-safe gratin dish, butter the bottom, then layer the cauliflower, cover with the sauce, bread-crumbs, grated cheese, and the remaining butter.

Bake in a low heat (less than 120C or 250F) oven for 10minutes, then put under the grill (or on the top rack of the oven with a higher heat) to brown for 5 minutes.

You can make this a very special dish by adding 200g (1 ½ cups) peeled shrimp. Cauliflower goes beautifully with the delicate flavor of shrimp.

The Larzac Gratin

For 6 people

1.5 kg (3 lbs) potatoes
150 g (a generous cup) Roquefort
10 cl (1/3 cup plus 2 tablespoons) crème fraîche or sour cream
40 cl (2 cups) milk
1 egg yolk
grated cheese for topping
oil, salt and pepper

Peel and slice your potatoes in thin rounds. Heat the milk. In a a double boiler over hot water (or in a microwave) melt your roquefort cheese with the cream and the egg yolk.

Grease an ovenproof deep dish pan and lay a layer of the potatoes to cover the bottom. Salt and pepper. Cover with half the cheese and cream mixture. Lay another layer of the potatoes, using them all up. Cover with the rest of the cream/cheese mixture. Pour the hot milk over it all. Salt and pepper, sprinkle with the grated cheese.

Bake in a hot oven (190-240C (350 – 450F)) for an hour.

A sheep house on the Larzac Plateau

An Onion Gratin with Roquefort

For 6

750g (1 ¾ lbs) onions - minced
100g (1 cup) Roquefort
6 slices of stale bread
nutmeg
grated cheese (usually gruyère)
olive oil
salt and pepper

In a saucepan, sautée the minced onions in oil till lightly colored. Add 2 litres (2 quarts) boiling water, and cook covered for 20 minutes.

Salt, pepper, and grate a bit of nutmeg over the onions.

Take a deepdish ovenproof pan and line it with the stale bread. Sprinkle on the Roquefort, pour the onion broth over the bread and cheese, sprinkle with grated cheese, and bake in a hot oven (190-240C (350 – 450F)) for 15 minutes.

The king of cheeses is honored with the king of vegetables! You can improve your onion broth with a glass of cognac should you wish.

Fresh Coco Beans Rouergate Style

For 4 people

500 g (1 ¼ lbs) fresh coco beans
(can be replaced by white beans, see below)
fresh sausages
1 slice of country ham diced
150 g (1/2 cup) minced bacon
1 tomato - peeled, seeded and chopped finely
1 garlic clove - crushed and minced
1 onion minced
1 bouquet garni
goose fat, salt and pepper

Put the coco beans a large stockpot. Add cold water to cover and bring to a boil. Let cook over a low flame for 5 minutes, drain and put aside.
In a heavy casserole with a lid (such as a Creuset/dutch oven) brown the onions, along with the bacon and ham in the goose fat. Add the chopped tomato. Continue to stir and add in the beans, the minced garlic and the bouquet garni. Cover with water and cook covered for an hour and a half over a low flame.
Add the sausage, putting it deep inside the beans, salt and pepper and continue cooking for another ½ hour.

Check the texture of the beans for doneness, and continue cooking or remove it from the heat.

A dish guaranteed to succeed. It is even better with two duck confit thighs put in among the beans from the beginning.

If using dried beans

Follow the recipe above, but first, soak the beans over night in water and extend the cooking time for a ½ hour to an hour depending on the age of the beans.

Best with beans no more than a year old.

Green Beans Rouergate Style

<u>For 4 people</u>

600 g (1.5 lbs) green beans
150 g (1/2 cup) smoked bacon chopped finely
vinegar
goose fat or olive oil
salt and pepper

Put the washed green beans into a saucepan filled with salted cold water. Bring to a boil and cook till tender (6-20 minutes depending on your personal preferenc and their size). Drain.
In a frying pan over a low flame, brown the bacon in the goose fat or oil, add the beans, salt and pepper and drizzle with the vinegar.

Mix, sautée a minute, then serve.

A simple and light dish, drizzled in the traditional Aveyron manner with a bit of vinegar.

Green Beans with Tomatoes

For 6 people

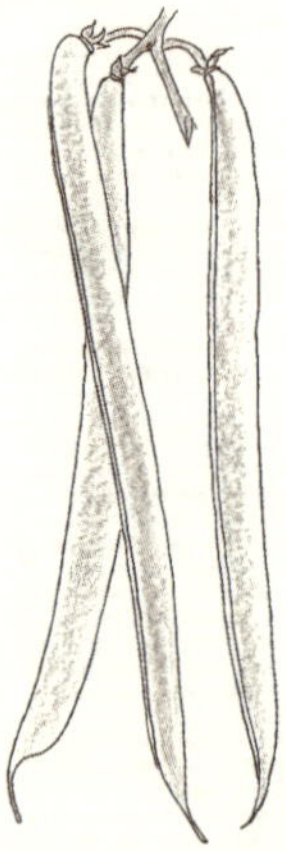

1.5 kg (3.5 lbs) green beans
4 tomatoes - peeled, seeded and quartered
1 garlic clove (not peeled)
1 good looking onion - minced
1 bouquet garni
goose fat or olive oil
salt and pepper

In a heavy bottomed casserole with lid, brown the onion, add the tomatoes. Next add the green beans, the whole garlic clove not peeled, the bouquet garni, salt and pepper. Cook over a low flame for 40 minutes.

A dish rich in vitamins with products fresh from the Southern Aveyron.

Duck Confit with Sorrel

For 6 people

2 duck thighs confit
2 kg (4.4 lbs) fresh sorrel leaves
6 eggs
1 cup vegetable broth
salt and pepper

Hard boil the eggs in salted boiling water for 8-9 minutes. Chill with cold water. Remove the shells and put aside.
In a heavy bottomed casserole with lid, warm the duck confit over a low flame in its fat for about 10 minutes. Put aside and keep warm.
In the duck fat, add the sorrel, salt and pepper, and cover with the egg whites sliced and crumbled.
Put the egg yolks in a mixing bowl and crush coarsely with a fork, moisten with the vegetable broth. Pour this mixture over the sorrel and blend gently. Cook over a low flame for 10 minutes.

Serve the sorrel with the duck confit.

The delicate acidic flavor of the sorrel is a perfect match to the richness of the duck confit.

Potatoes à l'étouffée

Smothered Potatoes

For 6 people

1.5 kg (3.5 lbs) potatoes
(try to find the bintje or charlotte varieties)
goose or duck fat or peanut oil or lard
salt and pepper

Peel and slice the potatoes thinly.
In a heavy bottomed deep-dish frying pan melt your chosen fat, and add the potatoes. Brown over a high flame.

Then lower the flame, salt and pepper and continue cooking for about 20 minutes or till tender.

Once the cooking time if finished, you can add a tome of fresh cheese cut in cubes. The sharp flavor of a tome is a good complement to potatoes. Should there be leftovers, don't hesitate to add them to an omelet.

Duck Confit with Potatoes

For 4 people

2 Duck thighs confit
600 g (1.5 lbs) potatoes
(try to find the BF15, or the belle de Fontenay)
2 garlic cloves
1 bouquet of parsley, salt and pepper

Dice the potatoes. Make a « persillade » by chopping the parsley leaves and the garlic finely (a rocking chopper/mezza luna is an excellent tool for this) and blend.
In a frying pan over a low flame, warm the duck confit in their fat for about 10 minutes. Put aside and keep warm.
Put the diced potatoes into the frying pan with the duck fat, salt and pepper. Cook for 15 minutes, stirring occasionally to prevent sticking, but let brown. Sprinkle with the persillade, and serve alongside the duck confit.

Potatoes with Cèpe mushrooms

For 6 people

1.5 kg (3.3 lbs) potatoes (bintje, monalisa or manon)
700 g (not quite 2 lbs) Cèpes/boletus (fresh)
1 garlic clove - minced
1 bunch of parsley - minced
a heaping tablespoon of goose fat, salt and pepper

Slice the mushrooms relatively thinly (1/4 inch). Slice the potatoes into thin rounds.
In a heavy bottomed deep-dish frying pan melt the goose fat and add the potatoes. Cook covered for 10 minutes. Turn the potatoes to let them brown on the flip side, salt and pepper.
Add the sliced mushrooms, the parsley and garlic and continue cooking over a low flame for 10 minutes.

Oven-baked Potatoes

For 4 people

1.2 kg (2 lbs plus) potatoes
200 g (7 oz) thinly sliced lard
(or fatty bacon if unable to find)
2 garlic cloves - minced
200 g (1 cup) minced onion
1 bay leaf
3 pinches of thyme
oil, 20 g (a heaping tablespoon) butter
salt and pepper

Peel and slice the potatoes into thin rounds.
In a greased oven-proof dish, put a layer of the potatoes on the bottom, letting them overlap.
Lay half the lard over the potatoes. Sprinkle atop the garlic, onions, thyme and bay leaf. Add the rest of the potatoes, and cover with the other lard slices.
Salt and pepper and a few dollops of butter.
Pour about a 1/2 litre (1 pint) hot water into the dish. Bake in a hot (190-240C (350 – 450F)) oven for 15 minutes.

Lower the heat and continue cooking for about 45 minutes or till the potatoes are tender.

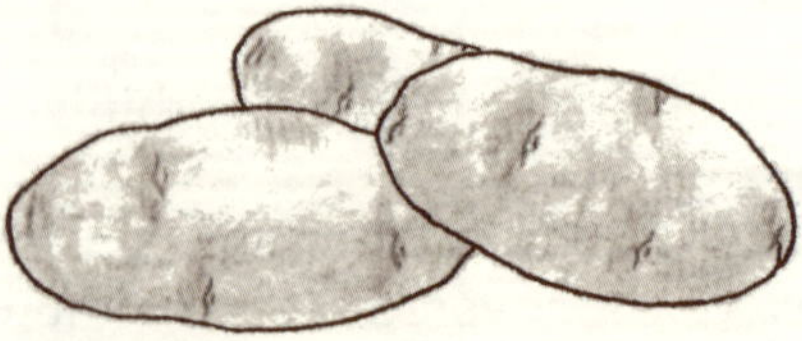

Stuffed Potatoes

For 4 people

1 kg (2.2 lbs) potatoes
250 g (8 oz) sausage meat
or shredded leftover stew meat
100 g (3.5 oz) Swiss chard greens
1 egg
1 garlic clove
1 onion
25 cl (1 cup) chicken stock
1 nugget of butter
salt and butter

Blanch the Swiss chard greens in salted boiling water for 3 minutes. Remove and drain. Put aside.
In a mixing bowl add the sausage meat, the egg, and the chard greens chopped finely, salt and pepper.
Slice the tops off the peeled potatoes. Carve out an inner cavity, and fill till heaping with the stuffing.
In a heavy bottomed casserole with lid, brown the onions and garlic in the butter. Lay the potatoes in the casserole snuggly (using the potato tops as necessary). Cover with any left over stuffing. Moisten with the chicken stock.

Cook covered over a low fire for approximately one hour, keeping an eye on the liquid level and adding more water as necessary.

A delicious childhood memory.

Ash-cooked Potatoes

Potatoes
Warm ashes from the fireplace or grill

Wrap the potatoes in aluminum foil and put them into the warm ashes. Wait at least a half hour. They should be soft to the touch.
The cooking time varies depending on the heat of the ashes. You can put hot coals on top of the ashes to speed up the cooking.

The aluminum foil is optional. It protects the skins from being burned. The delicate smoked flavor of the potatoes is delightful plain or with cheese.

Potatoes and Eggs Cooked Under the Ashes

Potatoes
Very fresh eggs
Salt and pepper
Warm ashes from the fireplace or grill

Follow the recipe as detailed above. Once the potatoes are cooked, cut off the top of the potato, and gently dig out a cavity. Break an egg inside it, salt and pepper and put the top back on the potato. Re-wrap in the aluminum foil, and cook over the coals for 5 minutes.

Rustic, fun, and delicately smoked!

Zucchini/Courgette and Ham Quiche

For 6 people

One pie shell
3 small zucchini/Courgettes
200 g (7 oz) thickly sliced ham
4 eggs
3 tablespoons crème fraîche (or heavy cream)
1 tablespoon flour
1 half litre (1 pint) milk
100 g (one cup) grated cheese
oil
salt and pepper

Blind bake your pie shell for 10 minutes.
Slice the zucchini/courgette in thin rounds, and dice the ham.
In a frying pan over a low flame, lightly brown the zucchini/courgette and the ham in the oil. Pour onto the pie shell, and sprinkle with the grated cheese.
In a mixing bowl, blend together the eggs, the cream, the flour, the milk, salt and pepper. Pour this mixture over the zucchini/courgette and ham.

Bake in a hot oven (190-240C (350 – 450F) for 30 minutes or till lightly browned and risen like a soufflet.

Some don't appreciate zucchini/courgette as its flavor is so bland. But here, with ham and cream, even the kids will love it!

Stewed Sassafras

For 4 people

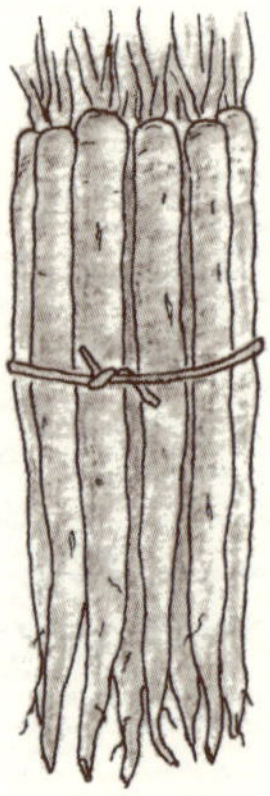

1 kg sassafras (2.2 lbs)
2 tablespoons tomata or pureed tomatoes
2 garlic cloves - minced
1 small bunch of parsley - chopped
50 cl (2 cups) chicken stock
flour
vinegar
duck fat or oil
salt and pepper

Wash and peel the sassafras. Cut them into two or three and soak them in water and vinegar till they blanch.
Wash well and drain.
Cut into 1-2 inch lengths. In a heavy bottomed casserole with lid, heat the fat and brown the sassafras. Sprinkle with the flour, then moisten with the chicken stock. Add a bit of water if necessary. Add the tomata, the garlic, the parsley, salt and pepper.
Cook covered over low heat for 15-20 minutes.

Use gloves when washing and peeling the sassafras as their skins can blacken your hands. This root vegetable with such a delicate flavor keeps well in a winter garden.

Sassafras with Parsley and Cream

For 4 people

1 kg (2.2 lbs) sassafras
1 small bunch of parsley chopped
1 lemon
1 cup chicken stock
20 cl (3/4 cup) crème fraîche (heavy cream)
nutmeg
salt and pepper

Juice the lemon and add to a bowl of cold water.
Place the sassafras into this acidulated water as soon as they are peeled.
In a saucepan, bring salted water to a boil. Put the sassafras into this water and cook for 10 minutes. Remove and drain, but keep warm.
Rince your sauce pan and pour in the chicken stock, bring to a boil, add the cream and continue cooking to reduce for 10 minutes. Salt, pepper, and grate the nutmeg a couple times over the sauce.
Place the sassafras on a serving platter, cover with the sauce, sprinkle with the parsley and serve.

This Rouergue vegetable is cited by Curnonsky in his book "the Trésor Gastronomique" as an excellent accompaniment to veal or chicken.

Tomato Tart

For 6 people

1 pie shell
5-6 tomatoes
200 g (7 oz) cheese
parsley
mustard
more grated cheese
or crumbled blue cheese
olive oil
salt and pepper

Spread a layer of mustard on the bottom of the pie shell. Lay slices of the cheese evenly over the mustard. Cover the cheese slices with tomato slices, aiming to fill in every hole.
Salt, pepper, and sprinkle with grated cheese and chopped parsley.

Drizzle olive oil over the top. Bake in a hot oven (190-240C (350 – 450F)) for 30 minutes or till nicely browned.

A quick and truly delicious dish!

Onion Tart

For 6 people

A pie shell
4 fat onions in thin slices
1 cup of tomata or tomato puree
100 g (1 cup) grated cheese
olive oil
salt and pepper

Brown the onions in the oil. Lay the onions in the pie shell. Cover with a thin layer of the tomata, salt and pepper and sprinkle over the grated cheese. Bake in a hot oven (190-240C (350 – 450F)) for 30 minutes.

Cooked onions are easy on the digestive system, and amongst its many virtues, they have selenium, a noted anti-oxidant.

Raw Tomatoes Stuffed with Roquefort

For 4

8 small grape tomatoes with their stems
200 g (7 oz) Roquefort
10 cl (1/2 cup) crème fraîche (sour cream)
salt and pepper

Cut the tops off the tomatoes, put aside. Dig out the inside of the tomatoes, salt lightly and turn upside down to draw out their juices.
In a small mixing bowl, mash the Roquefort with a fork, add the cream, pepper, and blend well.
Stuff the tomatoes, put their tops back on, and arrange on a serving platter.

Chill for 30 minutes before serving. It may be necessary to remove a sliver from the bottom of certain tomatoes to help them stand up neatly.

Quickly prepared and beautiful. These Roquefort filled tomatoes are a delight!

Roquefort balls

125 g (4.5 oz) Roquefort
1 tablespoon chopped celery
1 tablespoon chopped chives
60 g (4 tablespoons) sour cream
paprika

Blend the ingredients in a mixing bowl, and make small balls with your hands. Sprinkle with paprika. Chill before serving.

Curnonsky, an unconditional fan of the Aveyron and of Roquefort, prince-elect of gastronomy, created this recipe in honor of Rouergue.

« I never meet a tourist,
nor a gastronome without asking him
if he knows Rouergue »

Lettres de Noblesse 1935 Curnonsky

Aligot

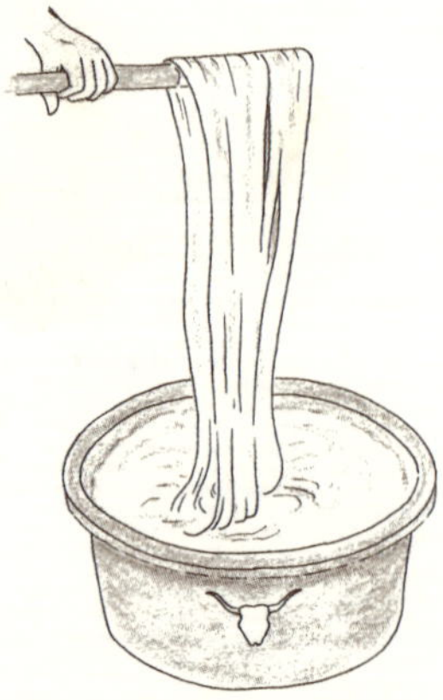

For 4 people

1 kg (2.2 lbs) potatoes
400 g fresh tome cheese (1 lb)
100 g (1/2 cup/1 stick) butter
250 g thick crème fraîche (sour cream)
1-2 garlic cloves (up to you) crushed and chopped

Peel the potatoes and quarter them. Then put them into a large sauce pan filled with salted water. Bring to a boil and let cook for 20 minutes. Check for tenderness with a knife.
Drain and rice the potatoes. In a heavy bottomed saucepan, over a low flame, incorporate the butter, the cream, and the garlic. Mix well with a wooden spoon.
Before serving, mix in the cubed tome cheese, mixing always in the same direction.

The aligot is ready to serve when you lift the spoon and a ribbon of melted cheese clings to the potatoes.

In the Aveyron, there are no great feasts without an Aligot. The Aligot is served very hot, and its preparation must be timed so the guests can participate. Invite your guests to help mix and test for the ribbon of cheese. The Aligot was born in Aubrac, and is now a staple on all the tables of the Aveyron.
The traditional dish to accompany grilled sausages or tripe in sauce.

Aligot with Bread

Soak stale sliced bread/baguette in milk. Drain and tap dry to remove excess milk. Then, make the Aligot above replacing the mashed potatoes with the bread.

Taureau Aubrac en bronze
Foirail de Laguiole

The Aligot with Bread is the ancestor of the current Aligot. It was dethroned by the arrival of the potato during the rein of Louis XVI. The monks of Aubrac used to serve it to the pilgrims on the route to Saint-Jacques de Compostelle. The hungry Jacquaires would ask in Latin, « something ? » « aliquid ? » which was later deformed with the passing years to aliquot, then adopted into the language of Langue d'Oc as aligot.

As a comedian once said, « we all need our aligot-elements ! »

Roquefort in Puff Pastry

For 6

A sheet of puff pastry
50g (2 oz) Roquefort
1 egg yolk

Slice the puff pastry into rectangles approx 2.5inx 5in. Garnish half the pastry with crumbled Roquefort leaving a bit of space on the edges. Touch a bit of water to the edges with your fingers or a pastry brush. Fold over the rectangles and pinch closed, raising the edges to prevent leakage.

Make a small design on the top pastry with the back of a knife (don't puncture). Brush with the egg wash, and bake in a medium hot (130-180C (260 – 325F)) oven for 10-12 minutes.

Lavogne, a reservoir for the sheep

Cheese from the Aubrac

A fresh tome of cheese from Aubrac
Eau-de-vie or marc made from grapes
Salt and pepper

In a canning jar, place slices of the tome, salt, pepper, and cover with the eau-de-vie/marc.

Close and forget for at least a month.

Roquefort Galettes

<u>For 4 people</u>

1 Leftover mashed potatoes (at least a quart)
75 g (2.5 oz) Roquefort
150 g (1 ¼ cup) flour
100 g (1 stick/1/2 cup) butter
a few walnuts

In a mixing bowl blend the flour, half the butter and the mashed potatoes till you get a smooth and even textured paste.
On a floured work surface, roll out the dough till thin. Cut circles of about 3 inches in diameter.
In a small bowl, mix together the Roquefort, the rest of the butter and the chopped walnut halves.
Take a circle of the dough, spread the Roquefort mixture on it and cover with another circle of dough. Place the galettes in a hot oven (190-240C (350 – 450F)) for about 15 minutes, or till the top is nicely browned.

Serve hot.

A tip : you can prepare these galettes the night before and either bake or re-heat them the day of your party.

Gatis de Saint-Affrique

Cheese Brioche

For 16 brioches

Brioche dough
250 g (2 cups) flour
10 g (1/3 oz) baker's yeast
125 g (1 stick plus 1 teaspoon) butter - room temperature
3 eggs plus 1 egg yolk to brush the dough
1 teaspoon salt
garnish
160 g (6 oz) fresh tome cheese
80 g (3 oz) Roquefort

Prepare the brioche dough the day before

Proof the yeast in a bit of warm water. Make a fountain in the flour and pour in the yeast, mixing gently together, add the eggs, and the salt. Work together till you get a smooth dough which doesn't stick to your fingers. Add the butter little by little, continuing to knead. Place the dough in an oiled mixing bowl and cover with a dishcloth. Let rise in a warm area away from any draughts.

The next day

Work the dough and cut it into 16 evenly sized balls.
Make a deep hole in each ball, and put a 16th of the tome in each, followed by a 16th of the Roquefort. Pinch the balls closed over the cheese. Cover the brioche with a towel and let rise for an hour in a warm corner of the kitchen.
Brush the tops of the brioche with the egg yolk wash, and bake in a medium hot (130-180C (260 – 325F)) oven for 30 minutes.

A gastronomic recipe enjoyed these past 100 years in Saint Affrique. The gatis is a true treat!

Rebarbe

Roquefort Cream with Eau-de-Vie

Leftover Roquefort
Milk (fresh/raw if possible)
1 cup eau-de-vie
pepper

Mash the leftover Roquefort with a fork into the milk. Pepper and add the eau-de-vie. Mix till you obtain a thick and unctuous cream. Chill for a couple days. Serve

The Pont Vieux and the Bell Tower of Saint Affrique.

Roquefort Soufflé

100 g (3.5 oz) Roquefort
4 eggs
60 g (1/2 cup) flour
30 g (2 tablespoons) butter
25 cl (1 cup) milk
salt and pepper

Separate the whites from the yolks. Whip the whites to a peak, firm.
In a saucepan over a low flame, melt the Roquefort and stir till smooth. Put aside.
In another saucepan, over a very low flame, melt the butter, add the flour and blend with a whisk. Pour in the milk and continue whisking. Remove from the heat and add the Roquefort, then the egg yolks one by one. At very last, add the whipped egg whites, salt and pepper.

Pour into a greased and floured soufflé mold. Bake in a hot (190-240C (350 – 450F)) oven for about 20 minutes, keeping a close eye on it.

Serve immediately.

Truffade

For 4 people

1 kg (2.2 lbs) potatoes
400 g (1 lb) fresh tome cheese
2 onions - minced
goose fat or oil
salt and pepper

Put the washed but unpeeled potatoes into a large sauce pan of salted water and bring to a boil. Let cook 20 minutes, remove, drain and cool before peeling and cutting into small rounds.
In a large frying pan, brown the onions in the goose fat.
Pour in the potatoes, salt and pepper. Cook over a low flame for about 10 minutes, or until very tender without being browned.
Add the tome cheese cut in small cubes, blend together with a spatula or a wooden spoon till smooth. Continue to cook till you can flip out the truffade like a large pancake.

Flip it out onto a plate and serve.

You can cook the potatoes the night before, and prepare them, peeling etc., the day of your feast.

The Retortillat of Aubrac

<u>For 4 people</u>

1 kg (2.2 lbs) potatoes - sliced in thin rounds
300 g (3/4 lb) fresh tome cheese from Aubrac
100 g (1/4 lb) laguiole cheese
parsley
oil
salt and pepper

In a frying pan over a medium flame, heat the oil. Add the potato rounds, salt and pepper. Cook covered over a low flame. Once the potatoes are cooked (about 20 minutes), add the fresh tome and the sliced laguiole.
Let melt over the potatoes and then gently stir together.

Sprinkle the chopped parsley over top and serve hot.

Buron de l'Aubrac

A traditional dish of the Aubrac buronniers, somewhere between an aligot and a truffade, brought up to date. You can add garlic or bacon as you please.

A Crown of Eggs with Ham

For 6 people

12 eggs
4 slices of ham
1 bunch of parsley
oil
salt and pepper

Grease a round cake tin. Line it with the ham slices. Break your eggs gently into the middle, so each yolk is visible. Salt and pepper and sprinkle with chopped parsley.
Place in a water bath and bake in a hot (190-240C (350 – 450F)) oven for 30 minutes. Check for doneness with a knife tip.
Chill before serving.

Guests are always amazed by the sight of this special dish. You can garnish the center with a dollop of mayonnaise, or tomata sauce, a bit of salad...

Eggs with Sorrel

For 4 people

6 eggs
400 g (1 lb) sorrel leaves
1 slice of country bread
milk
a nugget of butter
salt and pepper

Soak the bread in milk.
Hardboil the eggs in boiling water for 10 minutes. Drain, cool and peel. Mash the bread with two of the eggs.
In a frying pan over a low flame, melt the butter and add the sorrel, the remaining eggs quartered, and the bread mixed with eggs, salt and pepper.

Blend together with a wooden spatula. Heat for 5 minutes and serve.

Sorrel lends its slightly acidic flavor to the eggs and makes them easier to digest.

Eggs with Swiss Chard Greens and Spinach

Follow the above recipe but replace the sorrel with either spinach or Swiss chard greens. Serve with a small cup of tomato sauce to enhance the beautiful green of the dish.

The tomato's acidity replaces that of the sorrel.

Eggs Stuffed with Roquefort

<u>For 4 people</u>

5 eggs
30 g (2 tablespoons) Roquefort
1 teaspoon finely chopped celery
bread crumbs
oil
salt and pepper

Hard boil 4 eggs in a saucepan of salted boiling water for 8-9 minutes. Remove and cool with cold water, peel.
Cut the eggs in half.
Remove the yolks and mash with a fork into the Roquefort, adding the celery, salt and pepper. Fill the whites with the mixture. Put the eggs halves back together.

In a shallow dish whisk the remaining egg with a fork, dip the eggs in it, then roll in bread crumbs. Fry in oil for a couple minutes till lightly colored.

An Aveyron surprise best served with tomato sauce.

Eggs Under the Ashes

Fresh Eggs
Warm ashes from the fireplace

Moisten the eggs, then lay them gently under the ashes. Remove them when done – will depend on the heat of the ashes. Delightful if removed when just soft boiled.

In olden times these eggs were made especially for the young or the elderly. Eggs cooked without any excess expenditure of energy – as long as you have a fireplace or a barbecue!

Omelet Flambé

from Capou

For 4 people

12 eggs
1 glass of eau-de-vie
1/2 cup sugar

L'ami Capou

In a mixing bowl, beat the eggs together. Pour them into a large oiled frying pan and wait till the eggs have thickened a bit.

Mix the eau-de-vie with the sugar in a small saucepan and heat gently. Remove the omelet from the heat and pout on the alcohol/sugar mixture, light. Let flame as long as the alcohol remains, swirling it around to reactivate the flame. Once the flame dies, serve the omelet.

A desert delicious both as a main course or a dessert. This recipe was created by the famous «ami Capou» from Aubrac. He loved to entertain his guests by bringing out this flaming omelet. The alcohol burns off, but the flavors remain. Do be careful, and turn off both the fan above the burners, and limit draughts. Une recette autant appréciée en entrée qu'en dessert.

Omelet from the Grands Causses

For 5 people

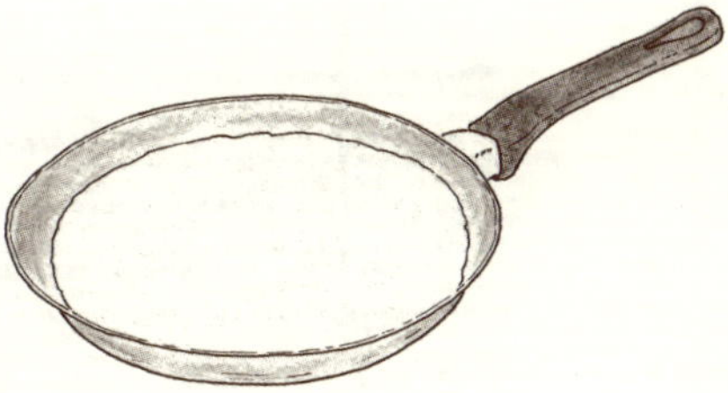

10 eggs
100 g (3.5 oz) blue cheese from the Causses
10 cl (1/2 cup) crème fraîche or cream
1 nugget of butter
salt and pepper

In a mixing bowl, beat the eggs with a fork (or whisk), salt and pepper. Crumble the blue cheese in a separate small bowl, blend with the cream.
In a frying pan over a low flame, melt the butter and pour in the eggs, add the blue cheese/cream mixture. Once the edges of the omelet are dry and the center cooked to your preference, slide it onto a serving plate and fold in half.
Serve hot.

A runny omelet, with the creamy cheese of the Grands Causses. There you have a lovely and delicately perfumed dish for a gourmet!

Snails Rouergate Style

For 4 people

4 dozen snails (ideally the small grey ones)
100 g (3.5 oz) sausage meat
2 slices ham - diced
1 garlic clove - minced
2 shallots - minced
50 cl (2 cups) dry white wine
1/2 cup eau-de-vie
1 nugget of butter
salt and pepper

In a heavy bottomed casserole melt the butter and stir in the minced garlic and shallots, then add the sausage meat, and the diced ham. Blend well. Moisten with the white wine (be sure to do so before the garlic burns !), salt and pepper. Cook covered for 30 minutes over a low flame. Add the snails and the eau-de-vie.

Continue to cook over a low flame for another 12 minutes to reduce the sauce.

For extra flavor and texture, you can add chopped walnut halves before pouring in the white wine.

Buttered Snails with Roquefort

For 5 people

5 dozen cooked snails
5 dozen snail shells or small pastries
100g (3.5 oz) Roquefort
5 garlic cloves
2-3 shallots
1 small bunch of parsley
100g (1/2 cup or 1 stick butter)
pepper

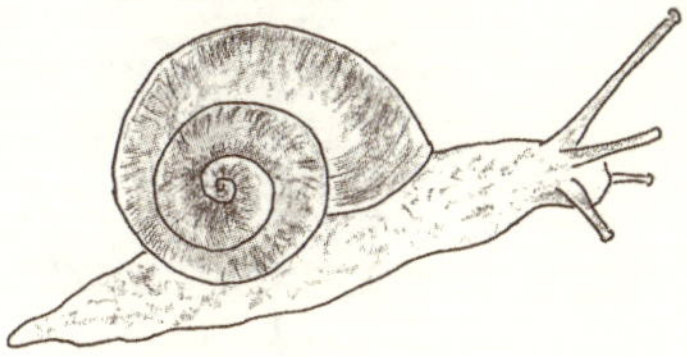

Finely chop the garlic cloves, the shallots, and the parsley. Blend the butter with the Roquefort, garlic, shallots and parsley. Put a bit of the Roquefort butter in the bottom of each shell, then a snail, then fill to the rim with the Roquefort butter, smoothing the surface.

Bake in a very hot oven (250C (over 500F)) for 5 minutes.

Be sure to firmly fill the shells so the snails are in contact with the rich flavors of the Roquefort.

Estofinado

For 8-10 people

2 kg (4.5 lbs) stockfisch (dried fish, normally cod)
500 g (1.25 lbs) potatoes
6 garlic cloves - chopped
1 large bunch of parsley - chopped
5 hardboiled eggs and 5 fresh eggs
10 cl (1/2 cup) milk
1 lemon
30 cl (1 ¼ cup) oil
pepper

The week before

Cut or saw the stockfish into 4 or 5 small pieces, put them in cold water and let soak for a week. Change the water daily.

The day of your feast

Put the softened stockfisch in a large stockpot, cover with water, bring to a boil and cook for 20 minutes.
Let cool in the pot for 20 minutes, then transfer to a colander to drain, keeping the water in the pot.
Add the potatoes in their skins to the pot and cook for 20 minutes.
While the potatoes cook, peel, flake and de-bone the fish.
Once the potatoes are tender, remove them, let cool. Then peel and mash them in a large pot.
Add the fish, the garlic, the parsley, the fresh eggs, the hard-boiled eggs cut in rounds, and the pepper.
Heat the oil, without bringing to a bubble and add to the fish/ potato blend. Mix all together with a wooden spoon over a high flame for 8-10 minutes. Then add the milk (heated) and the juice of your lemon.

Serve hot garnished with toasted croutons.

An emblematic dish from the Gorges of Aveyron and the Lot Valley. Almont les Junies made it a local specialty in the basin of Decazeville.

Each Aveyronnaise cook jealously keeps his personal balance of stockfisch to potatoes a secret. Certain prefer the name l'estofich' enriched with vegetables. Try inverting the proportions, such as 1 kg (2.2 lbs) potatoes to 250 g (2/3 lb) stockfisch. It is just as good!

The bell tower and front entrance
at the Place Notre-Dame de Villefrance-de-Rouergue.

Poorman's Estofinade

For 5 people

1 kg (2.2 lbs) potatoes
4 hard boiled eggs
3 fresh eggs
3 garlic cloves - minced
1 bunch of parsley - chopped
3 tablespoons crème fraîche (cream)
1 nugget of butter
30 cl (1 ¼ cup) walnut oil or another of equal quality
salt and pepper

In a large sauce pan, bring the potatoes to a boil in salted water. Cook for 20 minutes. Drain, cool, and peel.
Mash the potatoes in a large heavy bottomed casserole. Add the minced garlic cloves and parsley, the fresh eggs, the butter, cream, salt and pepper.
Heat the walnut oil and pour over the potato mixture. Stir over a flame for 10 minutes. Add the hard boiled eggs cut in 8ths.
Mix gently, serve hot.

There were times when even stockfisch was too expensive for the local farmers. But they knew how to make a delicious dish when they had to do without!

Stove Top Crayfish

For 4 people

24 crayfish
2 to 3 tomatoes - peeled, seeded and chopped finely
1 garlic clove - minced
1 shallot - minced
1 onion - minced
1 bunch of parsley
1 cup white wine
olive oil
salt and pepper

Clean the crayfish and remove the black bowel thread by cracking the inner shell of the tail and twisting to free it.
In a very large frying pan, heat the oil and then sautée the crayfish till red. Remove from the pan and put aside.

Pour more oil in the pan, and brown the onion, shallot and garlic. Add the tomatoes, followed by the crayfish and continue cooking covered over a low flame for about 10 minutes. Add the white wine, chopped parsley, salt and pepper. Continue cooking covered for about 6 more minutes over low heat.

This Rodez specialty from another era is both infinitely refined and marvelously flavorful. The delicate flesh of the crayfish should be savored, and - tradition dictates - brought to the mouth with your fingers! Be sure your guests have each a large napkin, and perhaps also finger bowls nearby.

Trout with Verjus

<u>For 4 people</u>

4 trout
1 bunch of unripe green grapes
1 garlic clove
1 bunch parsley
50 g (2 oz) bacon
chopped small
flour
oil, butter
salt and pepper

Make a « persillade » by chopping the parsley leaves and the garlic clove together. Put aside to sprinkle on the fish before serving.
Salt and pepper the inside of the trout, and fill with persillade and 4-5 grapes.
Generously flour both sides of the fish.
In a frying pan over a low flame, heat the oil, add the butter, the chopped bacon. Sautée a moment, then add the trout, frying 4-5 minutes per side.

Salt the trout on both sides. Before serving, sprinkle with remaining persillade and garnish with the remaining green grapes.

Verjus recipes are only possible during the season just before the grapes ripen. Out of season, replace the grapes with lemon slices.

Trout Meunière with Bacon

For 4 people

4 trout
100 g (4 oz) smoked chopped bacon
1 lemon
1 bunch parsley
flour
1 nugget of butter
salt and pepper

Flour the trout generously on both sides. Melt the butter in a frying pan over a low flame. Cook the trout in the butter 4-5 minutes per side, and put aside to keep warm.

Brown the bacon for 5 minutes in the butter. Salt and pepper the trout, drizzle the lemon juice over, followed by the melted butter. Garnish with the browned bacon and chopped parsley.

Trout from the rivers and streams, boraldes, in the region are the joy of the local residents of Espalion, Laguiole, Saint-Geniez-d'Olt, Rodez...

Alicot

For 4 people

1 kg (2.2 lbs or so) goose or duck giblets
(heads, necks, feet, wing tips, carcasses)
4 carrots - peeled and cut in rounds
2 tomatoes - seeded and chopped
250 g (2/3 lb) chestnuts
250 g (2/3 lb) sassafras root
- peeled and cut in rounds similar in size to carrots
1 onion - minced
1 bouquet garni
1 bouillon cube
goose fat, salt and pepper

In a large covered casserole, heat the goose fat, and brown the onion with the giblets. Add the tomatoes, cook for a few moments stirring from time to time.
Add the carrots and the sassafras.
Melt the bouillon cube in a half litre (a pint) of boiling water. Pour into the casserole, add the bouquet garni, salt and pepper.
Cover the casserole and prepare the chestnuts : slit the bottoms, boil in water and remove the two skins (both outer and the much thinner inner).

Put the peeled chestnuts in the casserole with the rest of the ingredients, and continue cooking covered over a low flame for 2 hours.

The Alicot has been promoted to « gastronomic treasure » in Rodez by Curnonsky, the prince-elect of gastronomy. Originally, the giblets would be put aside during the cleaning and preparation of various poultry. They were cooked separately, and woe be to he who fought over the head, or the wing tips..!
You can replace the chestnuts with cubed potatoes and a spoonful of flour.

Alouette en Robe des Champs (Lark in its field clothes)

Per person

1 alouette / field lark
1 large potato
goose fat or oil
salt and pepper

Pluck your alouette, remove innards, turn it over a flame to help remove any stray feathers, cut off its feet.
Salt and pepper both inside and out. Tuck its beak into the flesh above the breastbone. Remove a cap from your washed but not peeled potato. Remove much of the interior with a small spoon. Put some goose fat inside the potato. Place the alouette inside the potato and cover with the potato cap. Wrap the potato in aluminum foil.

Place under warm ashes in the fireplace or in a hot oven (190-240C (350 – 450F)) for an hour.

Delightful to behold, it's a bird in a pouch. However, do note, that in France, the only variety of alouette that you are permitted to hunt are the « alouette des champs ». If you'd prefer to not reduce the population of this bird, dear friend to all gardeners, then replace it with fresh sausage from the Aveyron or Toulouse.

Stuffed Pork Stomach

For 6 people

1 pork stomach
2 carrots cut in rounds
1 onion stuck with 2 cloves
1 bouquet garni, salt and pepper
For the stuffing
800 g (2 lbs) sausage meat
6 eggs
1-2 garlic cloves - minced
100 g (1/4 lb) stale bread
200 g (1/2 lb) pitted prunes
1 celery branch
young Swiss chard greens
1 bunch parsley
50 g (1/3 cup) flour, 25 cl (1 cup) milk
salt and pepper

Prepare the stuffing

Soak the stale bread in the milk. Chop the parsley, the celery, and the Swiss chard greens.
In a mixing bowl, blend together the sausage meat with the flour, eggs, bread (softened and squeezed of excess milk), the chopped greens, garlic, prunes, salt and pepper.

Fill the stomach, but do not overfill, and sew closed. In a large saucepan, bring water to a boil with the bouquet garni, the carrots, and the onion. Salt and pepper, and put the stomach in the boiling broth. Cook mostly covered for at least 2 hours.

This dish is truly Rouergat. Equally good cold or hot. The stomach can be served in thick slices, and even re-heated in a frying pan. And remember, this variation on the word ASE is not the one that means donkey! (ANE).

Astet de Najac

A Stuffed Roast Pork

<u>For 6 people</u>

1 kg (2.2 lbs) pork filet mignon
100 g (4 oz) salted bacon chopped
1-2 garlic cloves
1 bunch parsley
salt and pepper

Prepare the stuffing : chop the parsley and garlic finely, add the bacon. Slice the filet mignon in numerous places to make pockets. Salt and pepper. Fill the pockets with the stuffing and tie the pork together with string. Let rest 1-3 hours in the refrigerator. The meat will relax, and imbibe the flavors of the stuffing.

Roast in a hot (190-240C (350 – 450F)) oven for an hour.

Château forteresse de Najac

The stuffed pork filet can be enjoyed hot or cold, sliced. In olden times, the pork stomach was filled and roasted on the spit (aka the aste), from whence comes its name. The use of the string simplifies the work of the chef, and helps the advance preparation. The best of the best for a pork filet mignon !

Blanquette d'Agneau (lamb)

For 6 people

1 kg (2.2 lbs) lamb stew meat (the collar, shoulder, chest)
2 garlic cloves - crushed and chopped coarsely
1 onion - minced
1 bouquet garni
1 cup white wine
olive oil or goose fat
salt and pepper
Sauce
3 egg yolks
2 tablespoons flour
1 tablespoon crème fraîche
(cream or sour cream by your preference)
salt and pepper

If not already, cut the lamb meat into large bite-size pieces. In a large covered casserole, over high heat, brown the lamb in the oil and put aside.
Add more oil to the casserole and brown the onion. Moisten with the wine and a cup of water, add the bouquet garni, the garlic, the salt and pepper.
Bring to a boil, and add back in the lamb.
Cook covered over low heat for 30 minutes.
During this time, prepare the sauce :
In a mixing bowl, blend the egg yolks, the flour and the cream, the salt, pepper and extend with the cooking juices from the pot. Off the heat, add the sauce back into the casserole, blending well with a large spoon.

Let sit a moment covered till you are ready to serve.

Spring lamb is often served in this way with seasonal vegetables and garlic croutons to dip in the sauce.

Blood Sausage with Onions

For 4 people

500g (1 ¼ lbs) blood sausage
4 onions sliced
100g (4 oz) smoked chopped bacon
kidney fat or goose fat or oil
salt and pepper

In a frying pan, brown the onions in the fat with the chopped bacon. When the onions have browned, add the blood sausage cut in one-inch sections. Salt and pepper, cook approximately 5 minutes per side. Serve hot.

Blood sausage is delicious with apples, chestnuts, or celery rave, but it is with onions that it is at its best!

Bougnettes

1 pig's head cut in two
12 eggs
2 carrots - peeled and cut in rounds
1 garlic clove
2 onions stuck with 2 cloves each
1 bouquet garni
3 slices of bread
1 cup of milk
frying oil
coarse salt, salt and pepper

In a large heavy bottomed pot with a lid, place the pig's head, the onions, the carrots, the garlic (whole and unpeeled), the bouquet garni, salt and pepper. Cover with cold water.
Cook covered over a low flame for at least 2 hours.
During this time, soak the bread in the milk. Break the eggs into a mixing bowl and beat with a whisk or fork. Add the softened bread to the eggs, blend, salt and pepper.
Remove the pig's head from the broth. Drain and when cooled to a handling temperature, de-bone and dice the meat.
Add the meat to the eggs. Make apple-sized meatballs.
Deep fry in hot oil. They will come to the surface once they are cooked, approx. 30 minutes.

Remove the bougnettes with a strainer, and let drain on a rack before serving.

These can be enjoyed hot, cold, fried, in a soup...

Cabassol

Lamb's Head in its Broth

Per person

1 prepared lamb's head (i.e. cut in half, with eyes and muzzle removed)
2 carrots - peeled and cut in rounds
1 garlic clove - crushed and chopped coarsely
2 onions stuck with 2 cloves each
1 bouquet garni
1 handful coarse salt, pepper

Blanch the lamb's head in boiling water for 15 minutes. Clean the tongue by scraping it.
In a large covered pot, put the lamb's head, the onions, the carrots, the garlic, the bouquet garni, the coarse salt and pepper. Cover with cold water.

Bring to a boil, then lower heat and simmer covered for an hour (or a bit more).

A good head! Enjoy the ears, the tongue, the brains, the cheeks... with mayonnaise, mustard, pickled mushrooms, pickles... And don't forget the bouillon which has delighted many, including the prince-elect of Gastronomy, M. Curnonsky.

Duck Aveyronnaise

For 4 people

1 young duck
100g (1/4 lb) smoked chopped bacon
300g (3/4 lb) onions - minced
1 tablespoon flour
1 cup vegetable broth
2 tablespoons honey
duck fat
salt and pepper

In a heavy-bottomed pot with lid, brown the onions and bacon in the duck fat. Add the duck, salt and pepper and cook for 1 hour, basting periodically with the vegetable broth.
The duck is cooked when poked with a knife, the juices run clear.
Remove the duck from the pot, put aside and keep warm.
Meantime, add the flour to the pan juices and whisk. Add the honey, the salt and pepper. Put back over the flame and whisk till bubbling and browned.

Place the duck back in the pot and let sit 10-15 minutes covered before serving.

A duck prepared in the traditional manner, usually served with an apple marmelade.

Roast Duck

For 4 people

1 duck (about 1.5 kg or 2.5 lbs)
2 garlic cloves
sunflower oil
salt and pepper

Rub the duck with the oil and salt. Salt and pepper the interior cavity, and put the garlic – unpeeled – inside. Put the duck in a heavy-bottomed pot with lid with a half cup of water. Cook for an hour and a 1/2, turning the duck from time to time, and basting it with the cooking juices.
Add more hot water if necessary.

Quarter the duck, and serve.

The flavor of the duck is enough in this very simple and delicious dish.

Goat Kid with Sorrel

For 4 people

1 goat kid (shoulder, cutlets, leg)
1 kg (2.2 lbs) sorrel leaves
1 onion - sliced
25 cl (1 cup) vegetable broth
cream
oil
salt and pepper

Cut the kid into large bite size pieces, salt and pepper. In a heavy bottomed pot over a low flame, brown the onion in oil, then add the meat. Brown, then add the vegetable broth. Cook covered for 30 minutes. Cover the meat with the raw sorrel, and continue to cook for 10 minutes. Mix the sorrel with the cooking juices, and thicken the sauce with a couple spoonfuls of cream.

Serve hot.

Serve the meat lightly covered in the sorrel cream. Enjoy soaking up the delicious sauce with good country bread.

Rabbit Civet

For 6 people

1 large rabbit with its blood
125 g (4.5 oz) smoked bacon chopped
1 onion - sliced
2 garlic cloves - crushed
1 bouquet garni
1 pinch of nutmeg
3 tablespoons flour
75 cl (3 cups) red wine
vinegar, oil
salt and pepper

Put aside for later the liver and the blood with a drizzle of vinegar.
Cut the rabbit into serving size pieces. In a heavy bottomed pot, brown the onions and garlic in oil. Add the bacon, and the rabbit pieces.
Sprinkle in the flour, and stir forcefully till well colored. Add the red wine, and deglaze the pot with a wooden spatula. Add the bouquet garni, the nutmeg, salt and pepper.
Cook covered over a low flame for one and a 1/2 hours.
Grate the liver into a paste and blend with the blood. Take the rabbit meat out of the sauce and put aside. Keep warm.
Blend the liver and the blood with the sauce in the pot and warm over a low flame, stirring constantly. When it starts to bubble, lower the flame and continue to let cook, without boiling, for 5 more minutes.

Sieve the sauce and serve alongside the rabbit.

A dish with character! If you haven't any rabbit's blood on hand, you can replace it with a bottle of red wine and 10 g (1/2 oz) bitter chocolate. Dark chocolate replicates the texture of the blood. It colors the dish in a similar fashion, thickens the sauce, and brings just a touch of bitterness.

Wild Hare Civet

For 6 people

1 hare
100g (1/4 lb) chopped bacon
1 garlic clove, 2 tablespoons flour
vinegar, oil, salt and pepper
For the marinade
1 bottle red wine, 1 teaspoon dried thyme
1 bay leaf, 1 bouquet garni
2 carrots peeled and cut in rounds
1 garlic clove crushed, 2 onions sliced
1/2 cup eau-de-vie

Prepare the marinade the night before

Put aside the liver and the blood with a drizzle of vinegar.
Cut the hare into serving chunks, and put in a large bowl with the wine, the thyme, the bay, the carrots, the garlic, the onions, the bouquet garni, and the eau-de-vie. Stir from time to time. Being sure all the meat is well covered by the wine.

The day of your feast

Remove the hare meat from the marinade and drain. Filter the marinade and put aside. In a large heavy bottomed pot, brown the bacon in oil over a medium flame, followed by the hare till nicely colored. Sprinkle the flour in, let brown while you sitr with a wooden spoon. Pour the marinade over the meat and mix well. Salt and pepper. Continue to cook covered.over a low flame for an hour and 1/2.
Chop the liver and crush the remaining garlic clove, mash together and add the blood with a drizzle of vinegar. Pour this sauce into the pot and blend together 10 minutes before serving.

The civet is the ideal dish for an older hare. The older the hare, the longer it needs to marinate and cook to become tender.

Duck Confit

1 fattened duck (typically of the Barbary variety)
1 bay leaf
1 branch of thyme
coarse salt and pepper

<u>The night before</u>

Quarter the duck, separating the breasts, the thighs and legs. Cut away but keep the extra fat. Rub the meat with salt, pepper, and sprinkle with the bay and thyme. Refrigerate overnight.

<u>The next day</u>

Brush the salt off the duck.
In a heavy bottomed saucepan, melt the duck fat with a cup of water. Put the duck pieces into the pot and cook over a very low flame for 3 hours.
The confit is done when the meat is pricked with a knife and the juices run clear.
Place the duck into jars. Carefully separate the duck fat from the crumbs and juices in the sauce pan. Melt and pour over the duck till fully covered. Put your sterile lids on your jars.

Duck confit can be kept for months out of the light and in a cool place. Delicious served with white beans, sorrel or potatoes.

Coq au Vin from Marcillac

For 5 people

A good sized farm-raised rooster - cut into serving pieces
2 onions - sliced
100 g (1/4 lb) smoked bacon chopped
1 bouquet garni
4 slices bread
1 heaping teaspoon flour
75 cl (3 cups) red wine from Marcillac
1/2 cup Armagnac
1 nugget of butter
goose fat, olive oil
salt and pepper

In a heavy bottomed pot with a lid, over a low flame, brown the bacon, the onions, and lastly the rooster parts on all sides.
Pour in the Armagnac, heated beforehand. Flame carefully.
Add the red wine, the bouquet garni, salt and pepper. Bring to a boil. Let cook on high a couple minutes. Lower the flame to its lowest setting and cook for at least an hour (depending on the age of your rooster).
In a frying pan, brown the bread crumbled into small pieces in the olive oil to make croutons.
Make a beurre-mani with the flour and butter, and add to the juices in the rooster's pot to thicken at the end of the cooking period.
Serve hot with the fresh croutons sprinkled on top.

Drizzle your sauce brightened by the sunshine of Marcillac on your delicious rooster!

Stuffed Duck Neck

1 duck neck with a bit of the chest skin
200 g (7 oz) sausage meat
Swiss chard leaves
1 egg
1 small bunch parsley
1 garlic clove
50 cl (2 cups) stock
salt and pepper

Peel the neck skin delicately off the bone. Chop the meat that you remove from the neck. Put aside.
Blanch the Swiss chard leave in salted boiling water for 5 minutes. Remove and drain.
Make a persillade by chopping the parsley and garlic together.
Mix the duck neck meat with the sausage meat, add the egg, the Swiss chard leaves finely chopped, the persillade, salt and pepper.
Stuff the neck skin gently. Sew up the ends so no stuffing escapes during cooking.
Place the neck in an oven-safe pan with half the heated stock.

Cook in a medium hot (130-180C (260 – 325F)) oven for 1 hour, basting regularly with the cooking juices and the remaining stock.

A traditional Christmas dish. For an added touch, enrich the stuffing with bits of foie gras and eau-de-vie.

Coufidou de Millau

A Beef Daube (in wine sauce)

For 6 people

2 kg (4 ½ lbs) stew meat (collar, chest, cheek)
1 bottle red wine (from the Côtes de Millau if available)
200 g (7 oz) smoked chopped bacon
1 carrot peeled and cut in rounds
1 tomato peeled, seeded and chopped
2 garlic cloves
1 onion minced
1 onion stuck with 2 cloves each
1 bay leaf
2 tablespoons flour
oil, salt and pepper

In a large heavy bottomed pot, brown the meat cut in large chunks in the oil, add the minced onion. Sprinkle in the flour, and continue stirring. Add the garlic cloves, the other onion, the bay leaf, the carrot, the tomato and the bacon. Brown for a few minutes, then pour in the red wine, and if needed water to cover. Salt and pepper.

Cook covered for at least 3 hours.

A wonderful dish for the tougher pieces of the cow which become tender and delicious when prepared this way. This daube, and its many variations, is a must for Christmas in Saint-Affrique, cooked covered on a back burner for hours and hours...

Pork Trotters Daube

<u>For 4</u>

2 pork trotters cleaned and split in two
400 g (1 lb) pork belly (or bacon)
200 g (1/2 lb) bacon rind/skin
2 carrots peeled and cut in rounds
1 onion sliced
1 shallot sliced
1 bouquet garni
50 cl (2 cups) red wine
salt and pepper

Blanch the pork trotters in salted boiling water with the rinds for 10 minutes.
In a heavy bottomed pot, over a low flame, melt the fat of the pork belly/bacon cut in small pieces. Add in the shallot and onion and brown for a couple minutes.
Add the carrots, the bouquet garni, the blanched trotters, the rinds cut in thin strips, salt moderately and pepper.
Moisten with the red wine, pouring in enough to just cover the trotters.
Cook covered over a very low flame for 3 hours.
Add wine from time to time as necessary.

It is worth waiting for!

Wild Boar Daube

For 6 people

1 kg (2.2 lbs) boar shoulder or collar
3 carrots peeled and cut in rounds
1 onion sliced
1 shallot sliced
1 bay leaf
1 thyme branch
1 bouquet garni
10 juniper berries
1 bottle red wine
1 cup cognac
1 tablespoon flour
oil
salt and pepper

Prepare the marinade the night before

In a large bowl, put in the boar, cut into large bite-size pieces. Add the carrots, the onions and the shallots. Sprinkle in the juniper berries, the thyme and crumbled bay. Salt and pepper and pour in the red wine and cognac.
Stir from time to time to be sure all the meat is in contact with the marinade.

The next day

Remove the meat from the marinade, drain and tap dry. Filter the marinade and put aside.
In a large heavy bottomed pot, brown the meat in oil over a high flame. Lower the flame and sprinkle in the flour, stirring till the flour browns. Pour the marinade juices over top, add the bouquet garni, salt and pepper. Cook covered for 2 ½ hours.

A classic preparation for boar. It can be accompanied with fresh pasta or steamed potatoes.

Fallette

Stuffed Veal Breast

For 6 people

1 kg (2.2 lbs) de-boned veal breast
200 g (1/2 lb) sausage meat
lard strips (or bacon)
200 g (1/2 lb) smoked bacon chopped
1 egg
1 garlic clove
1 bunch parsley
1 slice stale bread
milk
salt and pepper

Soak the bread in the milk.
Make a persillade by chopping together the parsley leaves and the garlic.
In a mixing bowl, mix together the chopped bacon, the persillade, the sausage meat, egg, salt and pepper.
Slit open the veal breast without separating them. Lay the veal flat and cover with a layer of the stuffing. Roll up and tie together.
Bake in a hot oven (190-240C (350 – 450F)) for an hour and a half.

Oh how delicious and tender! If you have any greens (such as Swiss chard greens, spinach, salad leaves...) feel free to blanch and chop the greens to add to your stuffing.

Pan-fried Ground Meat Farçou

For 6 people

250 g (5/8 lb) sausage meat, or left-over beef shredded
200 g (1/2 lb) bacon
4 eggs
300 g (3/4 lb) Swiss chard greens
1 shallot
2 garlic cloves
150 g (1 cup plus 3 tablespoons) flour
goose fat or oil
salt and pepper

Blanch the Swiss chard greens in boiling salted water for 3 minutes, then remove and drain. Chop finely the blanched greens, the bacon, the shallot and the garlic cloves.
In a mixing bowl, blend together the sausage meat, the chopped mixture, flour, eggs, salt and pepper. If helpful, add a bit of water to help you bring the stuffing together.

Melt the goose fat, or heat the oil in a frying pan and spread out the meat mixture in the fat. Cook for 20 minutes on each side.

In the Aveyron farçous are very popular, be they lean or rich, hot or cold. They reflect the seasons. Traditionally, whatever local herbs are in season, growing in the herb garden, or along the country paths are added to the mix.

Lamb's Liver with Juniper Berries

For 6 people

1 lamb's liver
2 tablespoons crushed juniper berries
1 branch of thyme
10 cl (1/3 cup plus 2 tablespoons) cream
1 tablespoon vinegar
oil
salt and pepper

Slice the liver thinly, and salt and pepper. In a frying pan over a low flame, warm the oil and lightly brown the liver slices on each side. Put aside and keep warm.
Deglaze the pan over a high flame with the vinegar, scraping the pan with a wooden spoon. Add the cream, the juniper berries, the crumbled thyme, and stir well.
Pour the sauce over the liver slices and serve.

Lamb, thyme, juniper... breath the air of the Grands Causses!

Fricandeau with Herbs

For 5-6 people

300 g (3/4 lb) pork liver
300 g (3/4 lb) fresh pork bacon
1 pork caul fat
300 g (3/4 lb) Swiss chard greens
1 celery branch
1 onion
1 cup white wine
olive oil
salt, pepper

Soak the caul fat in room temperature water.
Blanch the Swiss chard greens in salted boiling water for 5 minutes.
Drain and cool, press the excess water out through a colander.
Chop finely the greens, celery, onion, liver, and the bacon. Salt and pepper.
Remove the caul fat from the water, dry it and cut it into 5 or 6 squares.
Make as many balls of the meat mixture as you've caul fat squares.
Wrap each in a piece of the caul fat, and place them side-by-side on a greased oven-safe pan.
Pour the white wine over them, with as much water, then drizzle with olive oil.

Bake in a hot oven (190-240C (350 – 450F)) for an hour, basting from time to time.

The fricandeau with herbs is but one of the many baked meat dishes known as farçous in the Aveyron.

Veal Fridandeau

For 6 people

1 cushion of veal about 800 g (2 lbs)
150 g (1/3 lb) smoked bacon (chopped)
1 carrot cut in rounds
1 onion cut in rounds
1 bouquet garni
50 cl (2 cups) vegetable broth
1 tablespoon cognac
1 nugget of butter
salt and pepper

In a heavy bottomed pot with lid, brown the bacon, and the veal. When the veal is nicely browned, add the carrots, onion, bouquet garni, salt and pepper.
Pour in the broth and the cognac.
Cook covered over a very low flame for 1 ½ hours, basting from time to time with the cooking liquid.

Before serving remove the fat from the pan juices and strain.

You can accompany the fricandeau with mushrooms tossed with parsley and garlic, or a sorrel purée.

Seven-Hour Leg of Lamb

Lamb with a spoon

<u>For 8 people</u>

1 leg of lamb about 2 kg (4.5 lbs)
3 carrots - cut in bite size pieces
2 tomatoes - peeled, seeded and quartered
2 onions - quartered
1 bouquet garni
30 cl (1 ¼ cup) vegetable broth
50 cl (2 cups) white wine
olive oil
salt and pepper

Salt and pepper the leg of lamb.
In a large heavy bottomed casserole with lid, over a low flame, brown the lamb on all sides in the oil.
Put the vegetables in around the lamb. Add the bouquet garni, salt and pepper.

Pour in the broth and the wine. Cook over a low flame for 7 hours adding water if necessary.

This is also called lamb with a spoon : it is so tender that you can cut it with a spoon. The cooking time is long, but the result is glorious !

Leg of Mutton stuffed with Garlic

For 5 people

1 Mutton leg of about 1,5 kg (3 lbs)
50 garlic cloves
1 onion minced
50 cl (2 cups) white wine
oil
salt and pepper

Salt and pepper the mutton.
In a large heavy bottomed casserole with lid, brown the mutton on all sides in the oil. Put aside.
Brown the onion in the pot, put the lamb back in, and add all the garlic cloves – whole and unpeeled. Pour in the wine.

Cook covered over a very low flame for 2 ½ hours, keeping an eye on the level of cooking liquid and adding water as necessary.

A dish that Gargantua would have enjoyed! The leg is served with garlic. For those who love garlic, they can spread it on good bread, or simply eat it as is.

Thrush on a Bed of Juniper

Per person

1 thrush
1 thin slice of fresh lard
(can be replaced with bacon)
1 slice stale bread
1 cube lard
1 shallot
5 juniper berries
1 nugget of butter
salt and pepper

Pluck the thrush, flame it and cut off its feet.
Remove the innards, putting aside the heart, liver and gizzards.
Salt and pepper inside and out.
Chop finely the lard, the heart, the liver, the gizzards, the shallot and crush the juniper berries.
Butter the bread, and then spread on this mixture. Wrap the thrush in the lard/bacon slice, and lay it atop the garnished bread.
Roast in a hot (190-240C (350 – 450F)) oven for 15 minutes.
Serve hot.

A rare dish these days. Our ancestors enjoyed roasted thrush whole! The thrush is naturally filled with the wild flavors of the juniper as it seeks out these berries in its diet.

Jambonneaux

7 pork shanks
3 kg (6 ½ lbs) pork shoulder
nutmeg
20 g (1 heaping tablespoon) salt and 1 g
(2 grates of a pepper mill) per kilo (2.2 lbs) of meat

Cube the meat to about a half inch (1 cm).
Weigh the meat and add a 1/3 cup water per kilo (2.2 lbs) of meat.
In a large mixing bowl blend the meats, a few grates of nutmeg, the salt and water.
Put into canning jars.
Sterilize the jars in boiling water for 3 hours.

Stuffed Jambonneau

1 pork shank
200 g (1/2 lb) sausage meat
nutmeg
salt and pepper

De-bone the pork shank. Season the shank and the sausage meat with the nutmeg, salt and pepper. Place the shank in a canning jar, pressed against the sides and leaving the interior empty. Fill the inside with the sausage meat.
Cover and sterilize for 3 hours.

Rabbit en "Cabessal"

For 8 people

1 rabbit approx. 2 kg
(4 ½ lbs)
50 cl (2 cups) vegetable broth
1 onion - minced
1 bouquet garni
1 cup white wine
olive oil
salt and pepper
for the stuffing
400 g (1 lb) sausage meat
one rabbit's liver
2 eggs
1 garlic clove minced
1 shallot minced
1 bunch of parsley - chopped
salt and pepper

Prepare the stuffing : In a mixing bowl, blend the sausage meat, the eggs, the chopped rabbit's liver, the parsley, garlic and shallot, salt and pepper.
Fill the rabbit with the stuffing and sew the cavity shut. Make two slices in the breast of the rabbit and place the front paws inside. In a large heavy bottomed casserole with lid, brown the onion in olive oil, and then place the rabbit on top. Add the bouquet garni, the vegetable broth and the white wine. Salt and pepper.
Cook covered over a low heat for 3 hours.

Serve the rabbit in the casserole. A slow-cooked dish enjoyed my many a Rouergat gourmet.

Rabbit with Mustard

<u>For 6 people</u>

1 rabbit, about 1.5 kg (3 lbs)
1/4 cup mustard
2 onions - minced
10 cl cream (1/3 cup plus 2 tablespoons)
1 cup white wine
oil or goose fat
salt and pepper

Cut the rabbit into portions, and rub them generously with the mustard.
In a heavy bottomed casserole with lid, brown the rabbit pieces till nicely colored but not burnt. Put aside.
Sweat the onions, and put the rabbit back into the pot. Pour in the white wine, and a cup of hot water, salt and pepper. Cook covered over a low flame for an hour.
Thicken the sauce with the cream and a teaspoon of mustard.

You can rub the mustard on the rabbit the night before and marinate it overnight to intensify the flavor.

Hare in Sharp Sauce

For 6 people

1 hare
oil
salt and pepper
The Sharp Sauce
1 ham neck muscle - chopped
the hare's liver
1 garlic clove - minced
3 onions - minced
5-10 juniper berries
1 bouquet garni
1 cup hare's blood
1 cup aged vinegar
1 cup red wine
duck fat
salt and pepper

To make the sauce

Put aside the hare's liver and a cup of hare's blood with a drizzle of vinegar.
In a heavy bottomed casserole with lid, sweat the onions in the oil or duck fat. Add the ham, the garlic, the bouquet garni, the juniper berries, salt and pepper.
Pour in the vinegar and wine. Let simmer gently covered for an hour, adding red wine as neçessary. Add the chopped liver to the sauce, and continue cooking for 10 minutes.
Remove the bouquet garni, and blend the sauce to smooth.

Add the blood with vinegar, and put the sauce in a double boiler over hot water.

Salt and pepper the hare, and put on an oven-safe dish. Drizzle with oil, and roast in a hot oven (190-240C (350 – 450F)) for 20 minutes (if you like it rare) or 35 minutes (for more done).

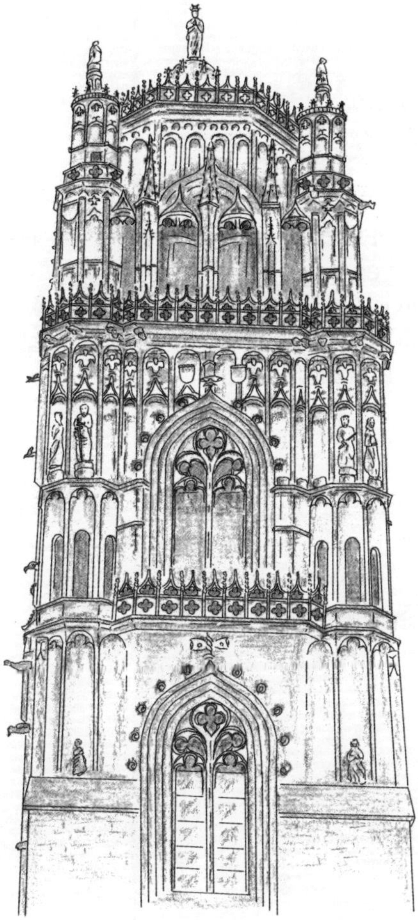

Rodez, la ville où l'on revient toujours

The hare is a dish to honor friends and family with the sharp sauce designed to accompany this royal dish. The proud hunter enjoys the hare roasted at the last minute, piping hot and rare.

Spit Roasted Hare "au Flambadou"

<u>For 6 people</u>

1 hare
fresh lard
olive oil
salt and pepper
a flambadou (see drawing)

Pour a cup of water in the drippings' pan beneath the spit. Rub the hare all over with oil. Turn the hare on the spit, basting it often with the juices caught in the drippings' pan below.
Heat the flambadou in the coals, put the lard into it. Let the lard drip as it melts and catch flame. Baste the hare with the flaming lard.
Continue cooking and turning for another 35-45 minutes. Hare is best served rare.
Baste again with the flaming lard, salt and pepper.

Carve the hare and serve with the sharp sauce (see the page 134).

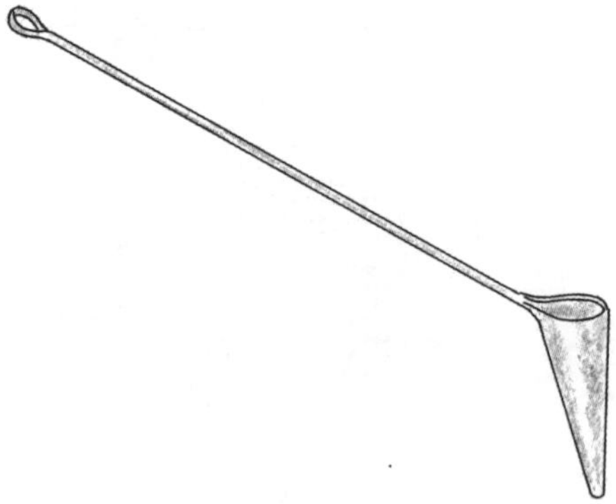

A hare is crusty on the outside and rare on the inside. That's how they like it in the Aveyron.
What the Southerners call a flambadou, the Northerners call a capucin. It is a metal cone with a hole on a long handle.

Melsat

4 eggs
300 g (3/4 lb) fatty bacon diced
100 g (1/4 lb) soft white bread
blood sausage casing (empty)
1 branch of thyme
salt and pepper

Moisten the bread with a bit of milk or water, then soak in the beaten eggs for 30 minutes. Mash the bread into the eggs with a fork, add the diced bacon, and crumble in the thyme. Mix together. Salt and pepper generously.
Fill the sausage casing, without over-filling. With string, mark the ends of each sausage.
Hang the sausages to dry in a cool, dry place (ideally a cellar...) for a few days.

Cook them in a soup or stew that isn't too thick.

The Melsat has long been a favorite for the long winters of the Tarn Valley.

Mourtayrol

Chicken in a Pot with Saffron

For 8 people

1 chicken
1 ham hock
1 kg (2.2 lbs) beef shin/shank
1 cabbage heart - quartered
8 carrots - peeled and cut into large pieces
8 potatoes - peeled and quartered
2 leeks - sliced in thin rounds
(whites and greens kept separate)
2 turnips - peeled and quartered
2 garlic cloves - crushed
2 onions, 2 cloves
2 doses of saffron or 4-5 filaments
1 bouquet garni
1 loaf country bread, salt and pepper

In a large dutch oven, bring 4 litres (4 quarts) of water to a boil. Add the onions stuck with the cloves, the garlic, the leek whites, the bouquet garni, salt and pepper.
When it comes to a boil, add the beef, the chicken and the ham. Cook covered over a low flame for 30 minutes.
Skim off the foam. Add the rest of the vegetables, excepting the potatoes, but including the leek greens. Continue to cook covered for another 2 hours.
Add the potatoes and cook for another 20 minutes.
Place the chicken and vegetables on a warmed serving platter.

Sieve the sauce, add the saffron, and pour into a soup dish well lined with bread.

Curnonsky calls this a gastronomic treasure of the Villefrance-de-Rouergue region. Tradition requires that you make a « chablot » with the broth. (Add a bit of red wine !).

Pork Liver Pâté

350g (nearly a lb) pork liver - diced to 1/2 inch (1cm)
250g (1/2 lb plus 2 oz) pork belly - diced to 1/2 inch (1cm)
200g lard
1 caul fat
2 eggs
1 shallot - minced
1 onion - minced
four spice mix
1 bay leaf
1 tablespoon cognac
flour, salt and pepper

Soak the caul fat in room temperature water.
In a heavy bottomed pot, gently melt the lard fat, lightly sweat the onion and shallot. Add the liver and pork belly.
Pour in the cognac, add the salt, pepper and four-spice. Add the eggs, and mix well with a wooden spoon.
Take the caul fat out of the water, and tap dry.
Lay the caul fat in a terrine pot with lid, allowing the edges to fall over the outside. Pour the pâté mixture into the caul fat. Fold the extra caul fat over the top to enclose the pâté. Place the bay leaf atop the enclosed pâté.
Make a simple dough with flour and water. Roll it out to a long rope and press the rope around the edge of the terrine pot. Place the lid firmly atop the dough to seal it.

Cook in a medium hot oven (130-180C (260 – 325F)) in a water bath for 1½ - 2 hours. Un-stick the lid, and place a heavy object atop the pâté to weigh it down.

You can always add chopped dried mushrooms to the mixture. As they moisten they will diffuse their rich aromas throughout the pâté. You can also replace the caul fat with strips of lard (or even fatty bacon).

Pork Liver Pâté with Foie Gras

Use the recipe on the page before, adding 150 g (5.5 oz) diced foie gras. Suggestion – keep the foie gras in the refrigerator till the last moment so the diced morcels are firm when mixed into the pâté. You don't need much foie gras to sense its presence and enjoy its flavor.

Ensemble château Renaissance
et Pont Vieux d'Espalion

Liver Pâté and Foie Gras are amongst the delicious specialties of Espalion.

Pastissous Rouergats

1 sheet puff pastry dough
125 g (4.5 oz) sausage meat
1 egg plus 1 egg yolk to brush on the pastry
1 garlic clove - minced
1 small bunch parsley - chopped
salt and pepper

Mix the sausage meat with the garlic, parsley, egg, salt and pepper.
Cut rounds in the pastry dough of about 10 cm (4 in) in diameter. Place a small ball of the meat in the middle of the pastry. Moisten the edges of the pastry with a bit of water. Fold the pastry over on itself to make a half moon shape. Pinch the edges shut.
Brush the top of the pastry with the egg yolk.

Bake the pastissous in a hot oven (190-240C (350 – 450F)) for 30 minutes.

These little pastries from Rouergate are a guaranteed success!

Partridge with Cabbage

<u>For 4 people</u>

4 young partridge
1 dark green curly-leafed cabbage
100 g (1/2 cup) chopped smoked bacon
4 lengths of thin lard
1 carrot - cut in rounds
1 garlic clove
1 onion - minced
12 juniper berries
20 cl (3/4 cup plus 2 tablespoons) vegetable broth
olive oil
salt and pepper

Remove the large outer leaves from the cabbage. Quarter it, and blanch in salted boiling water for 6 minutes. Remove, drain, and put aside.
Wrap the partridge in the lard strips. Heat the vegetable broth in a saucepan.
In a large heavy bottomed casserole with lid, brown the partridge on all sides in oil. Put aside.
Any burnt bits removed, and with fresh oil, brown the onion with the bacon, the carrot, the juniper berries, the drained cabbage, salt and pepper.
Put the partridge atop the cabbage, and pour the hot vegetable broth over top.
Cover and place in a medium hot oven (130-180C (260 – 325F)) for 40 minutes, depending on the age of the partridge.

Serve the partridge on their bed of cabbage, and drizzle with the pan juices.

A harmony of flavors from the Aveyron region.

Guinea Hen with Peas

For 4 people

1 guinea hen
1 kg (2.2 lbs) peas
100 g (1/2 cup) smoked chopped bacon
1 onion - minced
goose fat
salt and pepper

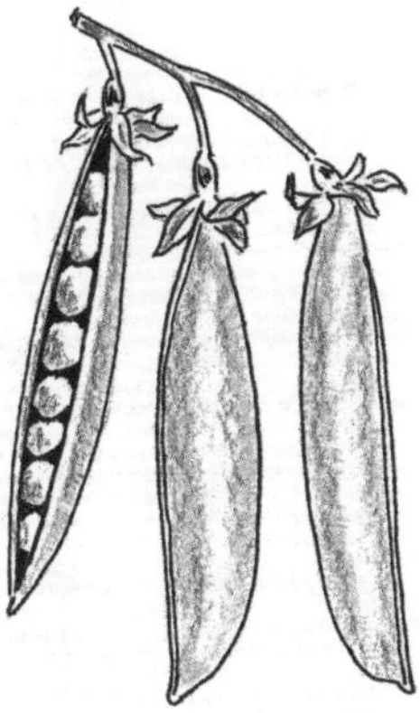

Rub the guinea hen in the goose fat and salt.
Place the hen in an oven-safe platter, and roast in a medium hot (130-180C (260 – 325F) oven for 45 minutes. Baste regularly with the pan juices and water if necessary.
In a frying pan over a high flame, brown the onion with the bacon, then add the peas. Cook covered over a low flame for 10 minutes
Add a cup of water to the guinea hen to extend the pan juices. Salt and pepper, then add the peas.
Continue cooking another 15 minutes.

Serve the guinea hen in its pot at the table. When you lift the lid the guests can breath in the aromatic steam as it wafts up. Curnonsky cites the guinea hen as a gastronomic treasure of Espalion.

Pot au Feu

For 4 people

800 g (2 lbs) beef or veal
(shank, belly, tail)
1 soup bone with marrow
2 turnips - quartered
4 carrots - cut largely
1 fennel root, or 1 branch celery
- cut coarsely
4 potatoes - quartered
2 onions stuck with 2 cloves
1 bouquet garni
salt and pepper

In a large dutch oven (or stock pot), over a low flame, heat 1 ½ litres (1 ½ quarts) water with salt. Add the soup bone.
Bring to a boil and skim. Add the bouquet garni and the meat. Cook covered for 40 minutes (if veal) or 1 hour 40 minutes (beef). Skim and add the onions, the fennel, the carrots, the turnips, the potatoes, salt and pepper.
Cook covered over a low flame for an hour.

Strain the broth and serve with the meat and vegetables, or chill and keep for the next lovely recipe.

Serve the meat hot with pickles and coarse salt. Serve the vegetables warm with a vinaigrette.

Pot au Feu Soup

The broth from your Pot-au-Feu (see above)
3 to 4 handfuls of vermicelli or pasta shells

Remove the layer of fat that congealed on the stock when chilled. Reheat the stock for 10 minutes. Add the pasta and continue to cook till the pasta is tender.

Chicken in a Pot with its Special Stuffing

<u>For 8 people</u>

1 chicken
2 liters (2 quarts) vegetable stock
1 onion stuck with 2 cloves
1 bouquet garni
<u>For the stuffing</u>
150 g (3/4 cup) sausage meat
a chicken liver - passed through a meat grinder or chopped very finely
a veal liver - passed through a meat grinder or chopped very finely
3 eggs
100 g (3.5 oz) stale bread
garlic, parsley, salt and pepper

<u>Prepare the stuffing</u>

In a mixing bowl, blend together the shredded bread, the eggs, chopped parsley and chopped garlic. Add the sausage meat, the livers, salt and pepper. Blend well with your hands till the paste is of even texture.
Stuff the chicken and sew it shut.
Bring the stock to a boil, add the onion and the bouquet garni. Place the chicken into the stock being sure it is completely submerged.

Cook covered over a low flame for 2 - 2 ½ hours. Check for doneness with a knife – when the juices run clear the chicken is done.
Carve the chicken and serve with its stuffing.

The stuffing can be served sliced hot with seasoned tomata, or cold with mayonnaise. You can replace the veal liver with ham.

Chicken Sautéed with Onions

Chicken Rouergat

1 chicken
5 onions
2 tomatoes (optional)
- peeled, seeded, and chopped
olive oil
salt and pepper

Cut the chicken into serving size pieces.
In a heavy bottomed casserole, brown the chicken in oil. Put aside. Over a low flame, lightly caramelize the onions in oil. They should sweat, but not in any way brown or reduce to a puree.
Put the chicken back in the pot, salt and pepper. Let simmer gently covered for 20 minutes.

Add the tomatoes and continue cooking for 10 more minutes. Serve.

This very popular Aveyron dish should be served quickly from the pan to best enjoy the rich aromas of the onions and chicken.
Even non-onion lovers enjoy this dish. Never use fewer onions. In general, there are never enough!
The South Aveyron region added tomatoes to the dish.
Quick and easy to prepare, it is the ideal dish for unexpected guests. And as the Aveyron folk enjoy entertaining...

Pounti

For 6 people

300g (3/4 lb) ham - diced
300g (3/4 lb) swiss chard greens
100g (1/2 cup) prunes
100g (1/2 cup) smoked chopped bacon
1 garlic clove - chopped
1 onion - minced
1 bunch parsley - chopped
1 bunch chives - minced
red wine, flour
a slice of bread, milk
For the batter
5 eggs
50cl (2 cups) cream
2 tablespoons flour
1 tablespoon baking powder, salt and pepper

Blanch the Swiss chard greens in salted boiling water for 3 minutes, drain.
Soak the prunes in red wine.
Moisten the bread with the milk.
In a frying pan over a low flame, brown the bacon, onion, and ham.
In a mixing bowl, beat the eggs with a fork, add the cream, the flour, the baking powder, salt and pepper. Add in the bread (having squeezed out the excess milk), the chopped greens and chives, garlic, parsley and the ham mixture.
Grease an oven-safe deep-dish pan, flour the prunes and lay them on the bottom of the pan. Then pour the mixture over top.

Cook in a hot oven (190-240C (350 – 450F)) for an hour, checking for doneness with a knife.

The pounti is a farçou from the Northern region of the Aveyron. The Swiss chard greens can be replaced by spinach, cardoon, lettuce, or enriched as you choose.

Lamb Sweetbreads with Sorrel

For 4 people

800 g (2 lbs) lamb sweetbreads
200 g (1/2 lb) young sorrel leaves
- washed and cut small.
1 lemon
20 cl (3/4 cup plus 2 tablespoons) cream
10 cl (1/3 cup plus 2 tablespoons) white wine
1 nugget of butter
salt and pepper

Put the sweetbreads in cold water for an hour, changing the water frequently.
Place a saucepan of cold water on a high flame. Add the juice from the lemon, and immerge the sweetbreads. Bring to a boil and lower the flame. Let simmer four minutes.
Remove the sweetbreads, cool them with cold water, and remove the skin, cartilage and fat.
Slice the sweetbreads in 1 cm (1/2 in) scallops.
In a frying pan over a low flame, melt the butter and brown the sweetbread slices on both sides. Salt and pepper and put aside to keep warm.
Pour off the excess fat, then deglaze the frying pan with the wine. Let simmer till reduced to half the volume. Add the cream, salt and pepper, and continue reducing by a third while stirring with a wooden spoon.
Add the sorrel leaves and keeping stirring and simmering for another 5 minutes.
Serve the sweetbreads with the sauce poured over them.

Sweetbreads' delicate nature makes them the king of the organ meats.

Rich Rissoles

100g (1/4 lb) pork - chopped
100g (1/4l b) sausage meat
100g (1/4 lb) fresh lard - chopped
1 egg
1 garlic clove - minced
1 bunch parsley - chopped
salt and pepper
<u>For your brisée dough</u>
500g (1 ¼ lbs or 4 cups) flour
3 eggs plus 1 egg yolk to brush on the dough
1 tablespoon baking powder
250g (1 cup plus 1 tablespoon) softened butter

In a mixing bowl, blend together the flour, the baking powder, add the eggs and the butter in small pieces. Work it till the butter is well distributed. As necessary add a bit of water to bring the dough together.
Let rest for 30 minutes in a cool place.
Mix the chopped pork and lard with the sausage meat, the garlic, parsley, egg, salt and pepper. Set aside.
Divide the dough in two and roll out in rounds. Place the meat mixture in the middle of one of the rounds, leaving about an inch (2 cm) around the rim clear. Moisten the edge with water and place the other round of dough on top. Pinch the edges shut.

Brush the top with the egg yolk, and bake in a hot oven (190-240C (350 – 450F)) for 30 minutes.

A delicious first course best balanced with a green salad. In earlier times it symbolized the Fat Monday festival in Rieupeyroux.

Salmis/Ragout of Pigeon

For 4 people

4 pigeons
4 slices of country bread
50 cl (2 cups) chicken broth
50 cl (2 cups) red wine
3 tablespoons flour
butter, olive oil
salt, pepper

In a heavy bottomed casserole, brown the pigeon in oil on all sides.
Heat the chicken broth. When the pigeons are nicely browned, add the wine, the broth, salt and pepper. Cook covered over a very low flame for 40 minutes.
Meantime, prepare a beurre-mani by mixing together 2 tablespoons butter with the flour.
Remove the pigeons and thicken the sauce with the beurre mani. Put the pigeons back in and continue to cook covered for 15 minutes.

Toast the bread. Serve by laying each pigeon on a slice of the toasted bread, the sauce on the side.

Pigeon is also known as the king's dish for its tender and delicious flesh.

Sanquette

Fried Seasoned Chicken's Blood

Fresh poultry blood
Stale bread
100 g (1/4 lb) bacon - chopped
garlic - minced
1 bunch parsley - chopped
vinegar
goose fat
salt, pepper

Using a shallow dish (or a shallow soup bowl depending on the quantity of blood), evenly distribute the crumbled bread, bacon, parsley and garlic in the plate. Moisten with the fresh blood to 2 cm (1 inch) thick. Salt and pepper. Let coagulate into a solid mass.

Heat the goose fat in a frying pan and slide the blood cake into the pan. Fry till deeply colored on either side. Check for doneness with a knife.

Drizzle with the vinegar and serve hot.

Known for its healthful benefits, you can serve this blood cake with pickles, salad...

Grandmother's Savory Tart

For 6 people

1 brisée dough, 1 puff pastry dough
250g (a generous cup) ground lamb
150g (2/3 cup) ground beef
3 tomatoes - sliced in rounds
2 eggs
1 tablespoon mustard
1 garlic clove - chopped
1 small bunch parsley - chopped
a pinch of thyme
100g (1 cup) grated cheese
1 tablespoon tapioca
oil, salt, pepper

Use the brisée dough for the bottom of your tart. Sprinkle the tapioca and the grated cheese on the dough.
In a mixing bowl, blend the ground meats, the mustard, the garlic, parsley, one whole egg, and one white (putting aside the yolk to brush on the top of the tart), salt and pepper.
Put this mixture in the tart shell. Cover with the tomato rounds. Sprinkle on the thyme, salt and pepper. Drizzle the oil over it all.

Place the puff pastry over top and pinch the edges together. Make slits on the top of the tart, brush with the egg yolk, and bake in a hot oven (190-240C (350 – 450F)) for 45 minutes to an hour, keeping an eye on the top crust so it browns nicely, but doesn't burn.

This savory tart with flavors from the Causses is a must. All your guests will enjoy it.

Tripade

For 4 people

1 fresh sausage (500 g or 1 ¼ lbs)
800 g (2 lbs) potatoes
500 g (1 ¼ lbs) sorrel leaves
2 eggs
a nugget of butter
oil, goose fat
salt, pepper

Cook the eggs in a pot of salted boiling water for 8-9 minutes. Cool with cold water and peel.
Peel and cut the potatoes into sticks.
Poke the sausage with a fork, and fry in an oiled frying pan on high heat for 7-8 minutes. Put aside and keep warm.
Pour off the excess grease, add the goose fat and fry the potatoes.
Salt and pepper and cook for 15-20 minutes turning them gently ever 5 minutes.
In a heavy bottomed saucepan, melt the butter, add the sorrel, salt and pepper, and cook over a low flame for 5 minutes.

To serve, lay the sorrel on a serving dish, cover with the potatoes, and place the sausage cut in 4 sections on top.

A simple rustic dish that has nourished many quite happily! You can replace the sausage with organ meats as you please, or stuffed gooseneck. Tripe for Sorrel is not to be confused with animal tripes (stomach).

Tripes with Saffron

For 6 people

2 kg (4 ½ lbs) blanched tripe
2 pork trotters
2 carrots - cut in rounds
1 tomato - peeled, seeded and chopped
1 head of garlic
3 onions - sliced in rounds
50 cl (2 cups) white wine
1g saffron
salt and pepper

Cut the tripe into squares approximately 5-6 cm (2 in). Quarter the trotters.
In a heavy bottomed casserole with lid, over a low flame, add the tripe, the onions and carrots, the garlic cloves (unpeeled), the trotters, white wine, salt and pepper. Cover with cold water.
Cook covered for 5 hours, keeping an eye on the liquid level.
Add the saffron, the tomato, and continue cooking for an hour.

The simplest of preparations for tripe and with Aveyronnais saffron of course!

Tripoux

2 mutton paunches
5 kg (11 lbs) veal caul membrane
Stuffing
500 g (1 ¼ lbs) salted lard - diced
20 garlic cloves - chopped
4 onions - minced
1 large bunch of parsley - chopped
salt and pepper
Broth
2 mutton trotters split in two
200 g (1/2 lb) pork belly, 1 bouquet garni
1 onion stuck with 2 cloves
1/2 cup white wine, salt and pepper

Preparation of the broth

In a large stockpot, add the mutton trotters, the pork belly, the bouquet garni, the onion with cloves, white wine, salt and pepper. Add 2 litres (2 quarts) water to cover.
Cook covered over a low flame during the preparation of the tripoux.

Preparation of the Stuffing

Blanch the veal membrane for 15 minutes, and drain. In a large mixing bowl, blend the diced lard, garlic, parsley, and onions. Add the chopped membrane, salt and pepper.

Cut the paunches into the scallops. Place a bit of the filling in the center and fold them over, sewing them shut. Add your packets to the simmering broth as they are done. Cook covered for 7-8 hours.

The tripoux are enjoyed all over the Aveyron, called «petites» in Espalion or «trenels» in Millau.
Certain still start their days with tripoux, made with mutton paunches and herbs.

Veal from the Aveyron and Ségala with Mushrooms

For 6 people

1 kg (2.2 lbs) veal shoulder
300 (3/4 lb) mushrooms (cèpes, porcini, chanterelles)
2 carrots - cut in rounds
2 tomatoes - peeled, seeded and chopped
1garlic clove - minced
1 onion - minced
1 bouquet garni
1/2 cup white wine
1 tablespoon flour
butter, oil
salt and pepper

Dice the veal into large morsels about 50 g (1.4 oz) each. In a heavy bottomed pot, over a low flame, heat the oil, add the butter, and brown the veal.
When nicely browned add the onion and sprinkle in the flour. Brown together.
Pour in the white wine, add the tomatoes. Add the salt, pepper, carrots, garlic, and the bouquet garni.
Cook covered for an hour, adding water if necessary.

Add the mushrooms whole or chopped depending on their size. Continue cooking for 10 minutes.

Veal from the Aveyron and Ségala is also a delight plain. It can be eaten simply with salt and pepper, and always lightly pink!

Desserts

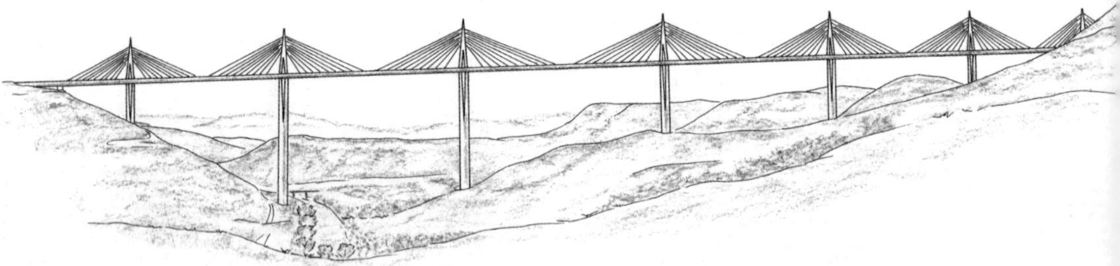

Acacia Flower Beignets

Fried dough

For 8 people

24 acacia flower clusters in full bloom
sugar
frying oil
For the batter
250 g flour (2 cups)
2 eggs
1 tablespoon olive oil
1 pinch of salt
1/2 cup water

Prepare the batter

In a small mixing bowl, put first the flour making a well in the middle, then the 2 egg yolks (putting the whites aside for later), olive oil, salt and enough water to blend to a thick cream consistency. Once blended, let sit an hour.
Whip the egg whites stiff, and gently fold them into the batter

Heat your frying oil. Dip each flower cluster into the batter and then drop it in the frying oil and let fry till lightly caramel colored. Remove with a strainer and place on paper towels to drain excess oil. Sprinkle sugar on top and serve hot.

The lovely acacia flower clusters are simply awaiting your harvesting hands to be enjoyed. Some find the batter improved with a couple drops of plum eau-de-vie. In France the Acacia tree is also known as the Robinier.

Biscotins

500g (4 cups) flour
200g (1/2 cup plus 6 tablespoons) butter
200g (1 cup plus 1 tablespoon) raw sugar
(or a mix of white and brown sugar)
2 packets of vanilla sugar (or 1 teaspoon vanilla extract)
2 eggs

In a mixing bowl, blend the flour, sugar, eggs and butter. Mix well till the dough comes together with no spare crumbs. Put aside and let rest 15 minutes.

Roll out the dough to about 2 cm (1in) thickness. Cut small squares.

Bake in a medium hot (130-180C (260 – 325F)) oven for 25 minutes – keeping an eye to remove them when just lightly browned.

These small cookies/biscuits have been a tradition in the Southern Aveyron for generations, particularly in Camarès. In olden times, they were made without butter.

Granmother's Clafoutis

For 6 people

500g (1 ¼ lbs) pitted cherries
150g (1 cup plus 3 tablespoons) flour
100g (1/2 cup) sugar
1 packet (1 tablespoon) baking powder
3 eggs
100g (1/2 cup) butter
1/2 cup milk

Butter a large deep-dish oven pan. Distribute the cherries evenly in the pan.
Melt the butter in a saucepan on the stove. Put aside.
In a mixing bowl blend together the butter and sugar, add the eggs one by one, then the flour and the baking powder.
Add the milk till the batter becomes fluid. Pour the batter over the cherries. Bake in a medium hot (130-180C (260 – 325F)) oven for 45 minutes.

The cherries from Aguessac are particularly wonderful due to the qualities of the earth and sun once allotted to vineyards, now given over to orchards.

Apple Clafoutis with Chestnut Flour

4 apples - cored, peeled and sliced
200 g (1 cup and 6 tablespoons) chestnut flour
3 tablespoons brown sugar
4 eggs
50 cl (2 cups) milk
oil

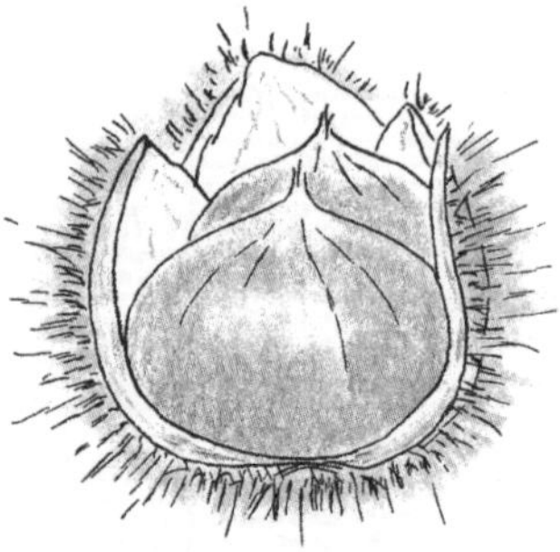

In a greased deep-dish oven pan, lay the apples overlapping on the bottom of the pan.
In a mixing bowl, blend together the eggs, and sugar. Add the flour and the milk and whisk till smooth. Pour the batter over the apples.
Bake in a hot (190-240C (350 – 450F)) oven for 40 minutes.

Clafoutis with Berries

You can use Grandmother's Clafoutis recipe and replace the cherries with the same volume of berries of your choice. Have fun and use more than one!

Chestnut Jam

For 1 kg (2.2 lbs) of purée

1 kg 200 g ($2^1/_3$ lbs) unpeeled chestnuts
750 g (1 lb plus 10 oz) sugar
1 vanilla bean

Score the base of the chestnuts and boil them for 3 minutes. Remove the 2 outer layers (both the thick brown hull, and the thin brown skin underneath).
Once cleaned, place the chestnuts in a saucepan of boiling water for 15 minutes. Drain the white chestnuts, and put them through a food mill to puree.
Put the puree into a jam basin (or a large heavy-bottomed sauce pan). Add the sugar, a cup of water, and the vanilla bean slit open its full length.
Cook over a very low flame for 20 minutes or so, stirring from time to time with a wooden spoon. Once the jam becomes a bit thicker, continue to stir a bit more till the jam becomes translucent. Pour into prepared jam jars.
Turn upside down to sterilize the lid.

This chestnut jam is wonderful on crepes, as a pie base, or simply by the spoonful. And remember, the chestnut is one of the greatest sources of potassium!
In nearly every French household you will find a large copper basin with two brass handles that is used exclusively for jam-making, be it for the figues from the wild fig tree in the yard, rhubarb from the garden, strawberries from the market...

Plum Jam with Vanilla

2 kg (4.4 lbs) pitted plums
1.5 kg (3.3 lbs) sugar
1 vanilla bean
1 lemon

The night before

In a large mixing bowl, place your chopped fruit with the sugar and the lemon juice. Open the vanilla bean and scrape the vanilla seeds into the blend. Then place the bean in the middle of the fruit. Cover with a cloth, and leave over night to permit the sugar to draw out the fruit juices.

The next day

Remove the vanilla bean. Pour the fruit into your jam basin (or large sauce pan). Bring to a boil, stirring from time to time. Continue cooking over a low flame for 30 minutes, scraping the sides and being sure to avoid any burn spots on the bottom. Do a jam doneness test (page 12) and, when ready, pour into your sterilized jars, cover and turn upside down.

Plum Jam with Oranges

Use the same recipe as above, but replace the vanilla with diced orange zest from one or two oranges. Be sure to avoid the bitter white pith.

Coupetado Rouergat

300g (3/4 lb) stale brioche (or challah)
250g (1 ½ cups) raisins
100g (1/2 cup) sugar
6 eggs
1/2 cup rum
1 litre (1 quart) milk
oil

Soak the raisins in the rum for at least a half hour.
Slice the brioche in 1 cm (1/2 inch) slices.
In a mixing bowl, beat the eggs with a whisk or fork, add the milk and sugar and mix well.
In a greased deep-dish oven pan, place a layer of brioche slices, filling in any gaps with extra bits of the brioche, pour the egg and milk mixture over top. Sprinkle with the raisins. Begin again. Finishing with a layer of brioche. Drizzle the remaining rum juice from the raisins over top.

Bake in a medium hot (130-180C (260 – 325F)) oven for an hour.

You can also use simple stale bread for this recipe.

Bonneval Chocolate Custard

For 4 people

200 g (1/2 lb) dark chocolate from Bonneval
30 cl (1 $^{1}/_{3}$ cups) milk
4 tablespoons corn starch

Break the chocolate into small pieces.
In a small bowl, whisk the cornstarch into the cold milk.
In a heavy bottomed saucepan, put 2 tablespoons water, and the chocolate. Melt while stirring constantly over a very low flame. When the chocolate is fully melted, add the milk and cornstarch and continue whisking till blended. When it begins to boil, remove from the flame.

Transfer to another bowl (or to individual serving bowls) and let cool.

This suave and flavorful custard is delightfully sinful accompanied by raspberries from the Aveyron.
The famous chocolate of Bonneval has been made by the monks of the Abbaye de Bonneval since 1878. The left-over chocolate from the factory is made into custards and cakes by the nuns to honor the Lord's day.

Crocande

450 g flour (3 2/3 cups)
100 g (1/2 cup plus 1 tablespoon) sugar
12 almonds or hazelnuts
1 tablespoon baking powder
1 egg yolk, milk
2 tablespoons orange blossom water
6 tablespoons oil

In a mixing bowl, blend the flour, the baking powder and the sugar, add the oil and the orange blossom water.
Work the liquids into the dry ingredients, and then add enough milk to bring together in a ball. Put the dough aside in a cool place to rest for an hour.
On a floured counter, either press or roll out the dough into a circle about 30 cm (12 in). Make a cross in the middle, raise the sides of the center towards the exterior to obtain 4 triangles. On the outside perimeter, make even cuts and fold one flap over another to mimic the sun's rays. Place a hazelnut at the base of each sunray.
With a pastry brush, paint the egg yolk liberally all over your sun.

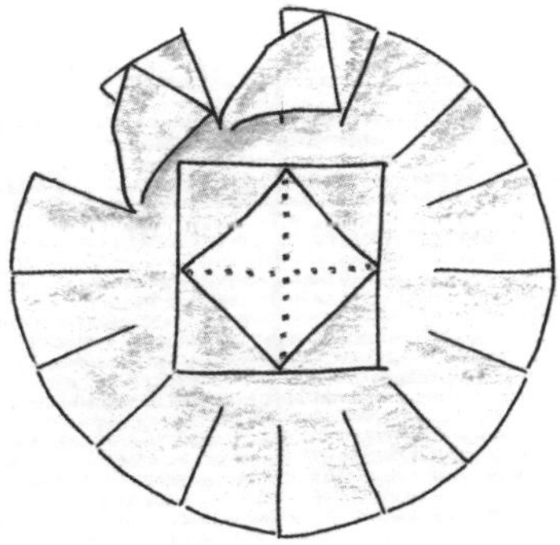

Bake in a medium hot (130-180C (260 – 325F)) oven for 20-25 minutes, keeping an eye on the color to be sure it doesn't brown.

The crocande keeps easily. It is particularly delicious when made with walnut oil or olive oil.

Old Time "Echaudé"

Chaudel with Three Corners

300 g (2 ½ cups pastry flour)
70 g (5 tablespoons) sugar
2 eggs
1/2 tablespoon baking powder
25 g (2 tablespoons) butter (melted)
3 g anise seeds or a bit of rum, eau-de-vie, liqueur...
salt

In a mixing bow, blend the flour, baking powder, sugar, anise seeds, melted butter, the eggs one by one, and the salt. Knead for a few minutes till all the flour has been incorporated.
On a well-floured work surface, press the dough out to about a 1/2 cm (1/4 in) thickness.
Using a cup or a glass, cut circles of about 6 cm (2.5 in) in diameter.
Take each circle and dividing it in three, pinch the folds together to make a three-cornered hat/wedge.
Bring a large saucepan of water to a boil. Slide the triangles into the water, keeping an eye on them so that they don't stick.
Once they come to the surface remove them with a strainer and place them on a dishcloth to dry.

Once well-dried, put them in a medium hot (130-180C (260 – 325F)) oven for 20-30 minutes to crisp.

These old time échaudés were prized by the pilgrims on the trail to Saintiago de Compostella as they wound their way through Podensis in the Aveyron.

Echaudés with Wine

Chaudel al vin

Old Time échaudés
Red wine (a young marcillac for example)
1/2 cup sugar

In a mixing bowl, pour in the wine, add the sugar and blend. Then add the échaudés. Let the échaudés absorb the wine.

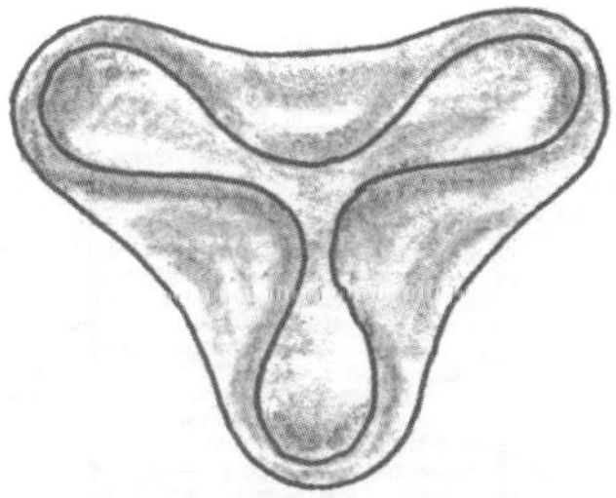

This pick-me-up was often enjoyed when taking a break during the strenuous harvest season. It has since become a tradition to « dip the cookies/biscuits ».

Flaune

1 pie crust
400g (1 lb) ricotta cheese
1 tablespoon flour
150g sugar (2/3 cup)
3 eggs
1/2 cup milk
2 tablespoons orange blossom water
lemon zest

Pre-bake your pie crust for 10 minutes.
In a mixing bowl, blend together the ricotta, sugar, eggs, milk, flour, orange blossom water, and lemon zest.

Pour into the pie crust and bake in a medium hot (130-180C (260 – 325F)) oven for 40 minutes.

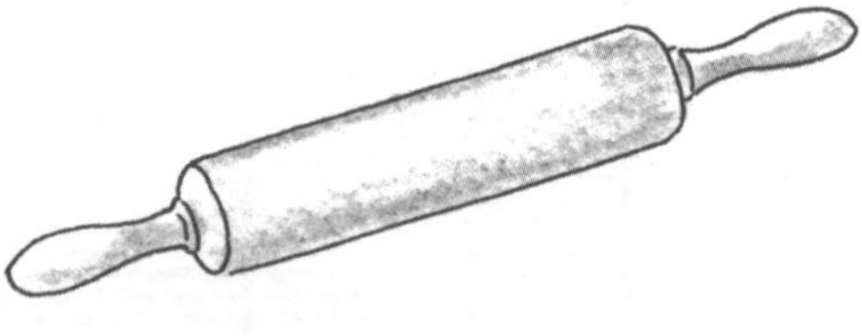

A typical dessert from the Southern Aveyron making use of the subtle flavors of sheep's milk ricotta. The ricotta is made from the whey produced during the fabrication of Roquefort. They whey is gently heated without boiling. The ricotta grains are remaining protein particles that float to the top where they can be skimmed off and put in a mold to drain.

Fouace

500 g (4 cups) flour
100 g (1/2 cup) sugar
30 g (1 oz) baker's yeast
3 eggs plus 1 egg yolk to brush on the pastry
2-3 tablespoons orange blossom water
100 g (1/2 stick) butter - melted
1/2 cup milk - warmed
a pinch of salt

The night before

Put the yeast into a glass of warm milk and gently mix to soften it. In a mixing bowl, blend the flour, sugar, salt and add in the softened yeast little by little. Continue mixing and add the orange blossom water, the melted butter, and the eggs. Mix well and knead for at least 10 minutes till smooth and elastic. Pat into a ball and put aside in a well-floured mixing bowl to rise.

The next day

Gently work the dough into a crown. Place on a lined and greased baking sheet. Brush the surface with the egg yolk and bake in a hot (190-240C (350 – 450F)) oven for about 40 minutes or till nicely colored.

The trick to making a good fouace is in the kneading, and in allowing for a good resting and rising of the dough. You need to give it time to grow, and in a temperature that encourages a steady rising (25C/77F). The fouace is served at all special occasions be they religious, personal, marriages, meetings...
In Laguiole, they keep aside a bit of the dough to make decorative additions to the fouace. In Najac, the city of pink sand stone, a gigantic fouace is paraded through the town during their August festival.

Chestnut Flour Fouace

200g (1 cup) Chestnut flour
300g (1 ½ cups) wheat flour
150g (2/3 cup) sugar
1 tablespoon baking powder
3 eggs
15cl (5 fl oz or approx 2/3 cup) milk
125g (4 oz) butter

In a sauce pan over a low flame warm the milk and melt the butter.

In a mixing bowl, blend the two flours, the sugar, and the baking powder, then add the eggs one by one.

Pour the milk an the melted butter into the bowl and blend together.

You can either use a baba baking dish (akin to small muffins) to make many small cakes, or roll out your dough and form a crown with it, placing it on a baking greased or nonstick baking tray.

Bake in a hot oven (190-240C/ 375-475F) for 40 minutes.

Cake on a Spit

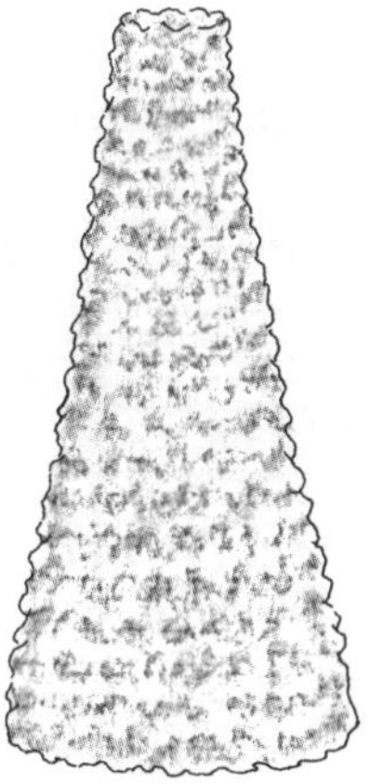

1 kg (2.2 lbs) flour
1 kg (2.2 lbs) butter
1 kg (2.2 lbs) sugar
24 eggs
100 g (1 cup) almond slivers

Melt the butter and put aside.
Separate the eggs.
In a large mixing bowls, mix together the egg yolks with the sugar, then add the flour, the melted butter. Mix till smooth.
Whip the egg whites till stiff, and fold them into the batter. Blend in the almonds.
Wrap the spit and the cone with a greased parchment paper. Place a dripping pan beneath to catch the batter drips. Turn the spit in front of the fire and pour the batter ladel by ladel over the cone. Wait between each ladel till the batter before has colored.
When all the batter has been used, let the spit turn till the cake is nicely browned.
And it's done!

This prestigious cake is still enjoyed in the local farmhouses. It requires the necessary equipment: the spit on which you can attach a cone. The cone is then positioned to be in front of the fire, on the hearth. Above the fire is placed a cast iron caldron that absorbs the heat of the fire and coals reflecting it evenly onto the cake.

Squash Cake

For 6 people

900 g (2 lbs plus) squash
(to obtain 500 g, 1 ¼ lb squash puree)
100 g (4/5 cup) flour
100 g (1/2 cup) sugar
4 eggs
2 tablespoons orange blossom water
a pinch of salt

Peel and chop the squash into small squares. Boil in a bit of water of water for 15 minutes, drain and puree by passing the squares through a vegetable mill or mixing in a blender.
Put the puree into a thick-bottomed sauce pan and cook over a low flame till the puree is smooth and thick.
Separate the eggs.
In a mixing bowl. Blend the flour, sugar, egg yolks, orange blossom water and salt.
Add the squash puree. Beat the egg whites till stiff and fold them into the batter.
Pour the batter into a greased cake pan.

Bake in a hot oven (190-240C (350 – 450F)) for 35 to 40 minutes till nicely risen and a knife comes out clean when testing the center.

Don't throw out the squash seeds. Toasted and salted they make an excellent appetizer or whenever snack.

A White Wine Cake from Entraygues

250 g (2 cups) flour
1/2 cup white wine from Entraygues
200 g (1 cup) sugar
1 tablespoon vanilla sugar (can be replaced by vanilla extract or vanilla bean)
3 eggs
1 tablespoon baking powder
1/3 cup oil

Separate the eggs.
In a mixing bowl, blend together the flour, baking powder, sugar, vanilla sugar, egg yolks, oil and white wine.
Beat the egg whites till stiff and fold into the batter.

Pour the batter into a greased cake pan and bake in a hot oven (190-240C (350 – 450F)) for 35-40 minutes.

This cake keeps well, its lovely texture as well. Just beat the egg whites well before adding them to the batter.

Walnut Tart

1 pie crust
1 cup chopped walnuts
1 cup sugar
4 egg whites - beaten till stiff

Ready your pie crust. In a mixing bowl, blend together the walnuts, sugar and egg whites. Pour into the pie crust, and bake in a medium hot oven (190-240C (350 – 450F)) for 30 minutes or till nicely browned.

Hearing the Aveyronnais speak so enthusiastically about their walnut tarts, how could this delicious dessert not have been invented here ?

Walnut Cake

(1 ½ cups) flour
180 g (1 1/3 cups) chopped walnuts
180 g (1 cup) sugar
180 g (3/4 cups) butter
3 eggs
1 tablespoon baking powder

Melt the butter. Separate the eggs.
In a mixing bowl, blend the flour, sugar and baking powder.
Add the butter, egg yolks, and walnuts.
Beat the egg whites till stiff. Fold them delicately into the other ingredients. Pour the batter into a greased cake pan.

Bake in a hot oven (190-240C (350 – 450F)) for 35 minutes.

Chocolate Chestnut Cake

For 6 people

600 g (1 ½ lbs) whole chestnuts
100 g (3.5 oz) dark chocolate
100 g (1/2 cup) sugar
100 g (1/2 cup or 1 stick) butter

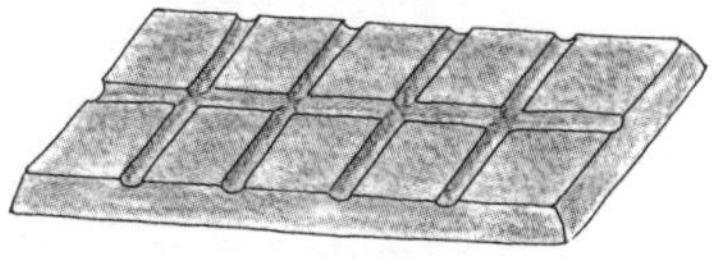

Score the bottoms of the chestnuts, and boil them for 3 minutes. Remove the two skins (outer dark brown, and inner lighter brown) at the same time if possible.
Bring a saucepan of water to a boil and put the skinned chestnuts in to cook for 15 minutes. Remove them from the pan, drain, and pass through a vegetable mill.
Melt the chocolate over a water bath, or in the microwave (in 30 second spurts to be sure not to burn).
Stir the sugar into a 1/2 cup of water till melted.

In a mixing bowl, knead together the sugar, chocolate, softened butter, and chestnut puree. Place in a mold and refrigerate till solid.

Chestnuts and chocolate go together wonderfully.

Rye Cake

Segali cake

<u>For 6 people</u>

130g (1 cup plus 1 tablespoon) rye flour
130g (2/3 cup) sugar
5 eggs

Separate the eggs.
In a mixing bowl, blend together the egg yolks and sugar. Add the flour.
Beat the egg whites till stiff and fold into the batter till the color is even.

Pour into your greased cake pan and bake in a hot oven (190-240C (350 – 450F)) for 30 minutes till nicely browned.

Rye is making a come back in our daily meals. It is both good for you and a pleasant change.

Quince Jelly

This recipe is made with ingredients left-over after making quince paste (p 187).

The seeds from your batch
of quince paste
The quince juice put aside
1 kg (2.2 lbs) sugar per liter (quart)
of quince juice

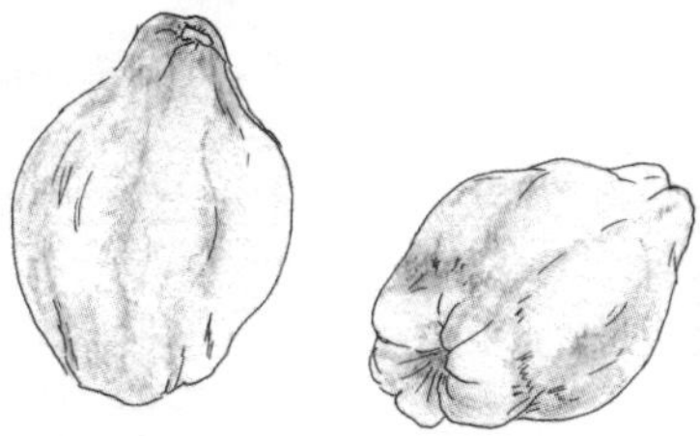

Cook the seeds in the quince juice for 10 minutes. Filter and measure out the volume of juice left over. Add the same weight of sugar as the juice. Add the sugar to the juice and put back in the saucepan to cook till the jelly takes. It will turn a lovely pink color.

Do the jam doneness test (p 12) and put into your clean jam jars.

A lovely jelly for crepes and morning toast. Children often prefer jellies before moving up to preserves.

Gimbelette

For 10 gimbelettes

500 g (4 cups) flour
100 g (1/2 cup) sugar
1 tablespoon baking powder
7 eggs
2 tablespoons orange blossom water
2 teaspoons anise seeds
50 g (3 tablespoons plus a wee smidge) softened butter

In a large mixing bowl, blend the flour, the baking powder, the sugar, and the anise seeds. Add the eggs, keeping aside one egg white. Add the butter and the orange blossom water. Mix well, and make a ball. Put aside to chill for an hour.

On a well-floured work surface, cut the dough into 10 even sized pieces. Roll each piece into a small rope and make crowns of these of about 12 cm (about 5 in) diameter, and 2-3 cm (1 in) thick. Set a saucepan of water to boil. When it begins to simmer, use a strainer and place the gimbelettes one by one in the water. When they rise to the surface remove and place on a cloth to drain excess water. Place side-by-side on a baking sheet and bake for 15 minutes in a hot oven (190-240C (350 – 450F)).

Beat the remaining egg white till not quite stiff. Brush the gimbelettes with the egg white, then sprinkle sugar over them. Bake for another 5 minutes.

Gimbelettes continue to be a traditional sweet in the Southern Aveyron, particularly during Easter.

Naines (which means dwarves)

The same recipe as above, but rather than making a round, cut the rope of dough into 12 cm (5 in) lengths, and cut to mimic a small person (see image here).

Massepain aka Montbazens

250g (2 cups) flour
250g (1 ½ cups) sugar
1 tablespoon vanilla sugar
(may be replaced with vanilla extract)
10 eggs
2 tablespoons orange blossom water
oil

Separate the eggs.
Whisk the egg yolks in a bowl, adding the sugar, vanilla sugar, and orange blossom water. Add the flour little by little.
Beat the egg whites till stiff and fold them into the batter. Bring the batter to a smooth consistency. Pour into a greased cake pan.

Bake in a medium hot oven (130-180C (260 – 325F)) for an hour, keeping an eye on it till nicely browned.

The massepain is often served during special family occasions, a fruit salad alongside, perhaps an île flotante, or simply with a glass of marcillac.

Oreillettes

Pigs' Ears

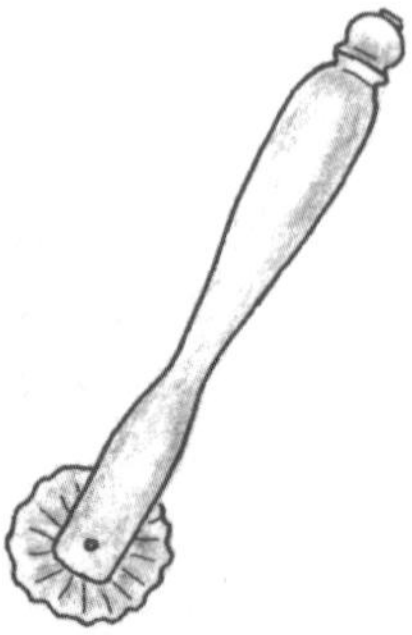

500g (4 cups) flour
3 eggs
the zest and juice of one orange
1 tablespoon orange blossom water
50g (3 tablespoons plus a smidge) melted butter
salt
oil, and frying oil
sugar for sprinkling on after frying

Put aside half the flour. Mix the rest with the eggs, the zest from the orange, the juice from the orange, the orange blossom water, butter and salt. Knead together adding the remaining flour little by little. Once the dough reaches a state of saturation and refuses to absorb more flour form it into a ball and put aside for an hour at room temperature.
On a greased work surface, roll out the dough to a thickness of 2 mm (not quite window pane thin). Cut squares of 5 cm (2 in) per side.

Prepare your frying oil and quickly fry your squares till golden. Remove and drain off excess oil on paper towels. Sugar as you wish.

These are just too good! Oreillettes are prepared for Mardi Gras and school parties. To make rolling out the dough a bit easier, you can always divide it into smaller portions.

Pain Perdu

French Bread

<u>For 4 people</u>

8 slices stale bread (2 cm or an inch thick)
25 g (2 tablespoons) sugar
2 eggs
25 cl (1 cup) milk
1 tablespoon orange blossom water
80 g (3/4 stick) butter

In a mixing bowl, beat the eggs, add the milk, the sugar and the orange blossom water.
Pour this mixture into a shallow dish. Dip the bread slices in the liquid, moistening both sides.
In a large frying pan, melt the butter and lay the moistened slices in the pan.
Gently brown each side for 5 minutes or so.

In the Aveyron, bread is never thrown away!

Plum Pastis

(Tart)

For 6 people

1 kg (2.2 lbs) plums
50 g (3 tablespoons) sugar
plum eau-de-vie
A sweet pie tart
300 g (2 ½ cups) flour
150 g (1 1/3 sticks) butter
(room temperature)
1 tablespoon sugar
a little bit of milk

In a large bowl, place the halved plums and drizzle the eau-de-vie over top.

Prepare the pie dough

In another mixing bowl, blend together the flour, sugar, and butter. Add a bit of milk to help the dough come together. Make a ball and put aside to chill for an hour.

Roll out your dough, and fill a pie mold, putting the excess dough aside.
Pre-bake the pie shell for 10 minutes. Fill with the drained plum halves. Sprinkle sugar over top, and drizzle a bit more eau-de-vie.
With the left over pie dough, make strips to form a criss-cross pattern on top.
Bake in a hot oven (190-240C (350 – 450F)) for 35-40 minutes.

Plums are everywhere in the Aveyron. They are full of minerals and very good for the digestion. You can also try this tart with a blend of apples and plums, interspersing them decoratively.

Pompet

For 4 people

4 ripe yellow-skinned quinces
100 g sugar
for the bread dough
400 g (3 $^1/_3$ cups) flour
20 g baker's yeast (2/3 oz)
1/2 cup milk
1 teaspoon sugar
1/2 teaspoon salt

Prepare the bread dough

In a large mixing bowl, blend together the flour, sugar, salt, and yeast softened with a 1/3 cup of warm water.
Add the milk little by little, and mix well, then knead till the dough is smooth and elastic.
Make a ball, place in a bowl and cover with a cloth. Let rise for at least 2 hours.

Prepare the pompet

Keand the dough and roll it out. Cut into 4 sections.
Remove the seeds and the heart of the quinces with the tip of a peeler. Blanch the quince for 10 minutes in boiling water, drain and wipe dry.
Fill them with sugar and completely enclose them in the dough.
Bake in a hot oven (190-240C (350 – 450F)) till the dough is nicely browned, about 40 minutes.

A great pick-me-up !

Pompe à l'huile

pompa a l'oli

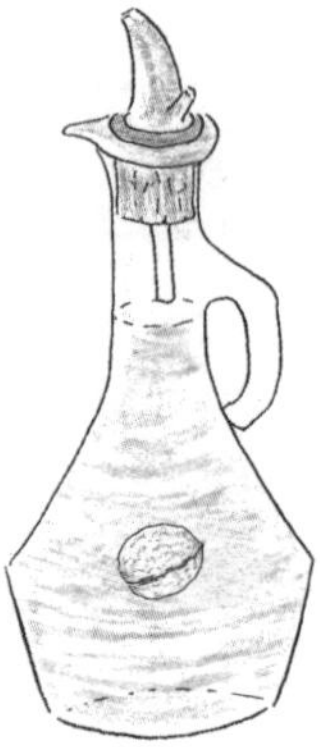

One batch of bread dough
(see the preceding page)
Oil (of good quality, olive..)
For the top
1 egg yolk
2-3 tablespoons walnut oil
walnuts (optional)
sugar

Prepare the bread dough.
Gently press out the dough on a greased parchment sheet to a one cm (1/2 inch) thick round. Raise the edges with your fingers.
Let the dough rise again.
Poke the dough all over with a fork.
In a small bowl, blend together the egg yolk and oil. Brush it over the dough. Sprinkle generously with sugar and chopped walnuts.

Bake in a medium hot oven (130-180C (260 – 325F)) for about 30 minutes or till nicely browned and risen.

A delightful treat for walnut lovers. The cooking time will depend on the rising : the more the dough rises, the better it will cook and the less hot the oven needs to be. Walnut oil is rather delicate and is best not over-heated.

Quince Paste

5-6 large quince
1 kg (2.2 lbs) sugar per kilo of cooked quince

The night before

Wash the quince, quarter, remove the seeds and put them aside in a small cheese-cloth pouch to make jelly (p 179).
Cut the quince into smaller pieces and place in a saucepan with water to cover.
Bring to a boil and blanch the quince for 10 minutes.
Drain the quince in a sieve over a bowl to catch the juice. Don't throw away the juice, but put aside to make jelly.

The next day

Puree the quince in a vegetable mill. Weigh it and add an equal weight of sugar. Heat the quince/sugar paste in a heavy bottomed sauce pan over a low flame for about 20 minutes stirring with a wooden spoon to avoid burning on the bottom. The color will become a lovely deep pink. When the paste pulls away from the sides of the pan, it is the right texture.
Pour out the paste and spread it out to a 1/2 in – 1 in thickness (1-2 cm).

The paste needs to dry over a few days and can be kept in a tin lined with parchment paper for a few months. Delightful nibbled in small squares or sticks.

Quince Jam

Use the same recipe as above, but cook for a shorter time and when the jam test (p 12) confirms its doneness, pour into sterilized jars and cover.

Prune Rissoles

500g (1 ¼ lbs) prunes
500g (4 cups) flour
100g (1/2 cup) sugar
1 tablespoon baking powder
3 eggs plus 1 egg yolk to brush on the top
250g (1 cup plus 1 tablespoon) softened butter

Soak the prunes in warm water or tea for 10 minutes. Remove them from the liquid to pit them. Pt the prunes back in the warm liquid for another 20 minutes at least to plump them.

In a mixing bowl, blend together the flour, baking powder, 80 g (1/3 cup) of the sugar, add the eggs, and softened butter in pieces.

Bring the dough together with a bit of warm water. Make a ball and put aside to chill for at least 30 minutes.

Drain the prunes, chop them finely, and add the rest of the sugar.

Spread out the dough and cut rounds of 15 cm (6 in) in diameter.

Put a layer of the prune mixture on half the round, leaving a small edge. Moisten the edge with water, fold over the other half and pinch the edges together, raising the edges a bit.

Brush the rissoles with the egg yolk.

Bake in a hot oven (190-240C (350 – 450F)) for 20 minutes.

As a variation, you can also chop up other dried fruits such as figs, apricots, or raisins with the prunes.

Strawberry Salad

For 4 people

1 kg (2.2 lbs) strawberries from Saint-Geniez-d'Olt
100 g (1/2 cup) sugar
25 cl (1 cup) wine (white or rosé)

Wash and drain the strawberries. In a large mixing bowl, blend the sugar and wine gently into the strawberries. Let marinate together for an hour, stirring gently from time to time.

Antoine Sannié, father of the Strawberry farmers of Saint-Geniez-d'Olt

Strawberry salad is excellent with a dry and fruity white wine, but also quite good with a rosé or a very young marcillac red.
Enjoy the richness of these strawberries, as well as the local know-how handed down by many generations in Saint-Geniez-d'Olt to tastefully fight weariness and stress.

The Marcillac Sun

500 g (4 cups) flour
250 g (1 $^1/_3$ cups) sugar
1 tablespoon baking powder
5 eggs
125 g (1/2 cup plus 1 tablespoon) butter
2-3 tablespoons orange blossom water
a pinch of salt

In a mixing bowl, blend together the flour, baking powder, sugar and salt.
Add the eggs, keeping one yolk aside to brush on top of the dough.
Add the butter, piece by piece, then the orange blossom water.
Knead together till your dough is smooth and elastic.
Make a ball and put aside in a cool place for a few minutes.
Press out the dough into a circle on a piece of parchment paper (the size of your baking sheet is ideal). Make a cross in the center. Lift up the triangles formed by the cross and fold them over towards the outer edge. All round, cut short straight lines to mimic sunrays. Fold these over in triangles, two by two. Brush the dough with the egg yolk.

Bake in a hot (190-240C (350 – 450F)) oven for 15-20 minutes or till nicely browned.

The cake from the sunny side of Marcillac.

Encalat Tart

For 6 people

1 pie crust
1 kg (2.2 lbs) cow's milk fresh cheese (yogurt can be used as well)
4 eggs
150 g (3/4 cup) sugar
3 tablespoons flour
2 tablespoons orange blossom water

Pre-bake your pie crust for 10 minutes.
In a mixing bowl, whisk together the flour, sugar, eggs, cheese/yogurt and orange blossom water.

Pour into the pie crust and bake in a hot oven (190-240C (350 – 450F)) for 45 minutes.

A Northern Aveyron classic created by a talented baker in Mur-de-Barrez.

Berry Tart

For 6 people

1 pie crust
600 g (1.5 lbs) raspberries, blueberries, currants, strawberries...
50 g (1/3 cup) buckwheat or other flour
100 g (1/2 cup) raw sugar
1 cup fresh cheese or yogurt

In a mixing bowl, blend together the cheese/yogurt, flour and 3/4 of the sugar. Spread this mixture on the base of the pie crust. Bake in a hot oven (190-240C (350 – 450F)) for 20 minutes. Remove the from the oven and spread the berries over the tart, sprinkle with the remaining sugar.

Put back in the oven for another 5 minutes.

This berry tart is easy and delicious to make over and over during the summer months. It never loses its charm.

Apple Tart with Chestnut Jam

1 pie crust
5 apples
100 g (1/2 cup) chestnut jam

Spread the chestnut jam evenly over the pie crust base. Peel and seed the apples, and slice them in thin half moons. Place the apples nicely over the jam. Bake in a hot oven (190-240C (350 – 450F)) for 35 minutes.

You can replace the chestnut jam with quince jelly or jam as you prefer.

Squash Tart

<u>For 6 people</u>

1 pie crust
900 g (2 ¼ lbs) squash (to obtain
500 g - 2 cups puree)
100 g (1/2 cup) sugar
4 eggs
1 orange (for its zest and juice)
3 tablespoons orange blossom water
25 cl (1 cup) milk
1 pinch salt

Pre-bake your pie crust for 10 minutes.
Peel, seed and dice coarsely the squash. Boil in a saucepan of water for 15 minutes. Drain and when cooled, pass through a vegetable mill to obtain the puree.
Put the squash puree in a saucepan with the milk, orange blossom water, and the zest and juice of the orange.
Stir and cook over a low flame till the puree is very smooth.
In a mixing bowl, whisk together the eggs with the sugar and salt. Pour the squash puree slowly into the egg mixture, whisking all the while. Pour the mixture back into the pie crust.
Bake in a hot oven (190-240C (350 – 450F)) for 30-35 minutes or till the center jiggles just a bit.

The squash is quite a surprising vegetable. It can make very good desserts.

Plum Tart

For 6 people

1 puff pastry
900 g (2 ¼ lbs) plums
sugar
corn starch or tapioca

Roll out your puff pastry and line your pie pan. Sprinkle on the sugar with the cornstarch or tapioca.
Halve the plums, pit them, and place them decoratively on the base of the tart.
Bake in a hot oven (190-240C (350 – 450F)) for 30 minutes.

Plum Puree Tart

For 6 people

1 pie crust
600 g (1.5 lbs) pitted plums
50 g (1/4 cup) sugar

Pre-bake the pie crust for 10 minutes. Put the plums in a blender and blend till smooth. Pour the puree into the pie crust, sprinkle with the sugar. Bake in a hot oven (190-240C (350 – 450F)) for about 30 minutes.

These are wonderful tarts from mid-August, making use of all that ripe fruit just waiting to be harvested. The Plum Puree tart can be even more delicious with the addition of eau-de-vie.

Hypocras

3 litres (3 quarts) tannic red wine, preferably aged in oak
800 g (2 lbs) candied sugar
spices
1 cinnamon stick
1 peeled ginger root
12 cloves
2 mace portions
1/2 nut of nutmeg
8-10 galanga beans (aka Siamese ginger)

Grate or crush the spices till in powder.
In a large saucepan (preferably stainless steel/non-reactive), pour in the wine and sugar finely crushed. Stir till the sugar is fully dissolved. Add the spices. Let cool and filter so that the wine is clear.

You will be delightfully surprised by the invigorating qualities of this medieval beverage. If you pass by Viala-du-Pas-de-Jaux on the way to visit the Knights Hospitalers, you may be served it.
The flavor of galanga resembles ginger.

Juniper Liqueur

1/2 cup green juniper berries
1 litre (1 quart) eau-de-vie (or other clear,
flavorless alcohol)
500 g (1 ¼ lbs) sugar

Put the sugar and the juniper berries in the eau-de-vie. Let macerate for at least 40 days, stirring from time to time to dissolve the sugar.

Filter and put in bottles.

An agreeable, woody flavor, with a good bit of character. Drink with moderation!

Ratafia

Red grape bunches
1 litre (1 quart) eau-de-vie
or other clear alcohol
(for 3 litres/quarts of grape juice)

De-stem the grapes. Crush and filter to obtain 3 litres / 3 quarts of grape juice. Pour both the grape juice and the alcohol into a large glass container (bonbonne in French). Macerate for 40 days, turning the bottle at least once a day.

Filter and put into small bottles.

To Friendship!
In Latin «Rata Fiat» means may our market exchange conclude!
Often served as a before-dinner drink, or at times with dessert. It marries beautifully with Roquefort.

Quince Ratafia

Quince Liqueur

1 litre/1 quart of quince juice (from about 6 ripe quince)
25 cl (1 cup) eau-de-vie (or other clear alcohol)
300 g (3/4 lb) sugar

Peel the quince, and grape them down to the seeds. Put aside for a couple hours. Put the gratings into a fine sieve or cheese cloth. Press to obtain the juice. Add the eau-de-vie and the sugar, respecting the proportions above.

Bottle and let rest in a dark place for about a month. Filter and bottle. Enjoy after two months, or two years!

This golden liqueur is a delight to the palate, and its color is like sunrays to the eyes.
All year long, keep a bottle around to heal any tummy aches. Quince Liqueur ages beautifully, but if your tummy aches...

Peach Leaf Wine

100 peach leaves
5 litres (5 quarts) white wine
1 litre (1 quart) eau-de-vie
1 kg (2.2 lbs) sugar
1 vanilla bean
5 bitter almonds

In a large recipient, pour in the white wine, the eau-de-vie, and add the peach leaves, the vanilla bean split down the middle, and the almonds. Close the container and let macerate 40 days. Shake from time to time.

Once the maceration finished, filter, add the sugar, dissolving it well before dividing into smaller bottles.

Wait another six months before tasting, and even more if you can. It will only improve!

Harvest the peach leaves between the two « Notre Dame » 15 August to 8 September, when they begin to turn. They will be at their maximum flavor.

The vanilla and almonds give a little extra kick that will shake a « my that's good! » from your guests.

But, don't tell them! It's your secret.

Walnut Wine

5 litres (5 quarts) good red wine
1 litre (1 quart) eau-de-vie
(or other clear alcohol)
40 green walnuts with their shells
1 kg (2.2 lbs) sugar
1 cinnamon stick

In a large recipient, pour in the wine, the eau-de-vie, the quartered walnuts, and the cinnamon.
Let macerate for 40 days in the closed recipient. Shake from time to time.

Filter the contents, add the sugar, and let rest for another 40 days. Bottle.

The festival of St. Jean (towards the summer solstice) marks the moment that walnuts are at their most flavorful and tannic. Be patient for at least six months for this beverage to be at its best.

Recipe Index